"Heather Davis Nelson has written a wonderful work on the topic of shame. She brilliantly weaves her own stories and those of others into the larger story of what God does with our shame. She fearlessly brings the light of Jesus to shine in the dark recesses of our souls as she helps to free us from the pain of shame."

> **Paul E. Miller,** Executive Director, seeJesus; author, *A Praying Life* and *A Loving Life*

"Most of us can quickly point to a shame story from our past—that moment when we believed that we were shunnable, rejectable, and maybe even despicable. We, as heirs of God, so often live with a low level of misery caused by shame, even though Jesus came to set us free. In her insightful new book, *Unashamed*, Heather Davis Nelson explores the chains that bind us and then reminds us that we're not just ex-sinners; we are saints who have been made new. Like a trusted friend, who also happens to be a therapist, Heather walks you to a place of freedom so you can be all Jesus intended you to be."

> **Susie Larson,** national speaker; radio host, *Live the Promise with Susie Larson*; author, *Your Beautiful Purpose*

"*Unashamed* proclaims that Jesus Christ secures freedom, honor, and glory for us and applies that truth to the many ways we all suffer shame. Because shame makes us feel naked, filthy, and excluded, we need to know the healing that comes from God's declaration that in Christ we are clothed, clean, and accepted into the family of God."

> **Justin and Lindsey Holcomb,** authors, *God Made All of Me*, *Rid of My Disgrace*, and *Is It My Fault?*

"It is difficult to understand shame apart from the gospel. This book is all about the great exchange: shame for beauty. It will flood your soul with life and give you a breath of fresh air. Heather has given all of us who counsel—and all of us who struggle—a gift."

> **Rod Mays,** Adjunct Professor of Counseling, Reformed Theological Seminary; Executive Pastor, Mitchell Road Presbyterian Church, Greenville, South Carolina

"Heather Davis Nelson speaks from an authentic heart on a subject too painful and embarrassing for most to admit they struggle with. *Unashamed* is much more than informative or inspirational. This book could be life-changing. Heather does a beautiful job uncovering the amazing story of grace and redemption, showing how Christ can break the endless cycle of shame that leaves so many in bondage. I highly recommend *Unashamed* for anyone who desires to live a life of freedom and hope found in Christ, and for anyone who desires to point others to see beyond their shame and live victoriously."

Monica Rose Brennan, Associate Professor and Director of Women's Ministries, Liberty University

"Heather Davis Nelson has made a significant contribution to addressing the critical topic of shame, which is often ignored or misunderstood among the people of God. I declare myself her debtor for the help her work has been to my own sanctification."

Joseph V. Novenson, Pastor, Lookout Mountain Presbyterian Church, Lookout Mountain, Tennessee

"*Unashamed* helped me see my misplaced shame and accept the freedom and love Jesus Christ offers me every day. I'm thankful for Heather's heart-felt approach. Here is a thoughtful, knowledgeable, and biblical work."

Trisha R. Wilkerson, author, *Everyday Worship*; biblical counselor

"Shame is a paralyzing, life-hindering reality we all experience. *Unashamed*, written by my dear friend Heather Davis Nelson, is not a book written primarily from her writing desk or her counselor's office. This book was written from her personal faith journey through shame as she has sought to abide in Jesus and his Word through tears, pain, and faith crises. This is what makes the book so powerful. This is why I recommend the book for anyone. It is a signpost to Jesus and his healing, transforming gospel."

Ellen Mary Dykas, Women's Ministry Coordinator, Harvest USA; editor, *Sexual Sanity for Women*

"Heather Nelson has refreshingly and freely brought to light a topic that isn't discussed much in Christian circles. I found myself breathing many sighs of relief as I realized I wasn't alone in my experiences of shame. Heather continually pointed me to the only One who can fully cover and release me."

Julie Courtney, Director of Women's Ministries, seeJesus

UNASHAMED

UNASHAMED

Healing Our Brokenness and Finding
Freedom from Shame

Heather Davis Nelson

WHEATON, ILLINOIS

Library of Congress Cataloging-in-Publication Data

Names: Nelson, Heather Davis, 1979– author.
Title: Unashamed : healing our brokenness and finding freedom from shame / Heather Davis Nelson.
Description: Wheaton : Crossway, 2016.
Identifiers: LCCN 2015046437 (print) | LCCN 2016007332 (ebook) | ISBN 9781433550706 (tp) | ISBN 9781433550737 (epub) | ISBN 9781433550713 (pdf) | ISBN 9781433550720 (mobi)
Subjects: LCSH: Shame—Religious aspects—Christianity. | Healing—Religious aspects—Christianity.
Classification: LCC BT714 .N45 2016 (print) | LCC BT714 (ebook) | DDC 248.8/6—dc23
LC record available at http://lccn.loc.gov/2015046437

Crossway is a publishing ministry of Good News Publishers.

VP		27	26	25	24	23	22	21	20	19	18	17	16
15	14	13	12	11	10	9	8	7	6	5	4	3	2	1

To Seth, Lucia, and Alethia,
without whose love and grace these pages would not exist,
for you have given me courage to stay on this journey.

Contents

Foreword

"Shame is everywhere," writes Heather. "Each emotion I feel gets connected or tainted with shame if I let it." She is right. It is everywhere, and it seems as though everything in life gets channeled through it. Yet it is so hard to talk about.

Shame has two conflicting instincts. It needs to isolate and hide, and it needs a community in which to be transparent. Hiding, of course, usually wins. It is the easier and more natural of the two. But we are savvy enough to know that the easy way is rarely fruitful, which leaves us with the hard way—and that seems impossible. Then, left with no viable option, we default back to hiding.

This is where *Unashamed* comes to our aid. Someone has to be the first to talk. Shame is pent up and just waiting for an opportunity to say something, but someone has to be the first to talk. Someone has to introduce a new culture that says, "We, as God's people, known and loved by him, are implored by God to speak openly from our hearts. So let's talk. I'll start." And Heather starts us talking. She speaks openly, and the rest of us feel free to follow.

Once we test the waters and begin to talk, we still need

direction. That elusive sense of being unacceptable needs help being more specific. With this in mind, *Unashamed* takes us to places in our past that affect us more than we know, and it guides us to the present where shame that connects to perfection, body image, performance, and parenting invades the details of our lives.

Through all this, *Unashamed* keeps taking us back to Jesus, the one who both knew shame and takes our shame. Without him, there would be no reason to bring shame into the open. With him, we are built up rather than torn down, shame is forced to retreat, and we notice the possibility of joy as we know and are known by the Holy One.

Ed Welch
Author, *Shame Interrupted*

Acknowledgments

I am indebted to my counseling professor Ed Welch, who first taught me about the distinction between shame and guilt during his class at Westminster Theological Seminary in 2006. I later read his in-depth treatment of shame: *Shame Interrupted*. Concurrently, I stumbled upon the TED talks of prominent professor and shame researcher Brené Brown on the topic of shame and vulnerability. Her books *The Gifts of Imperfection* and *Daring Greatly*, as well as the ecourse on *The Gifts of Imperfection*, further illuminated the role shame has had in my own story. This book stands on the backs of these two professors, and I hope to build on their work through my offering.

I am beyond grateful to my clients over the past decade who have entrusted their shame-laced stories to me, and whose courage in being vulnerable and walking through the darkness to get to the light has inspired me in my own journey out of shame. You have paved the way for me and many others.

Thanks to the "Unashamed Group" from the summer of 2015 for piloting the manuscript and giving me crucial encouragement and constructive criticism.

Thank you to my extended family, both near and far, who

has supported me and helped to make this book become a reality through your feedback, babysitting, and Marriott points: Mom and Dad, Fred and Joan, Jonathan and Nicole, Bryan and Megan, Grandma, aunts, uncles, and cousins. You have witnessed many of my most shameful moments and seasons of life, and you continue to love me and laugh with me through them.

This book is the culmination of dreams and ideas discussed over dinners, coffee, phone calls, and front porch conversations with many friends. I want to particularly thank the friends who offered invaluable insight and edits as they read portions of the first draft: Heather Byrne, Becky Buma, Maria Booth, Katherine Carrera, Beth Clarke, Julie Courtney, Jonathan and Nicole Davis, Katherine Donnithorne, Kelly Dwyer, Ellen Dykas, Erin Irwin, Lev and Karen Hojda, Kiran Lall-Trail, John and Christy Leonard, Lynette Landfear, Amie Patrick, Marty and Debra Paulaitis, Sally Proulx, Allyson Sabin, Robin Price Sanford, Jen Schaefer, Beth Schmidt, Anne Smith, Dan and Karen Thrush, Shelly Wagner, and Bob and April Willetts. Our church community at Trinity Presbyterian Church enthusiastically supported me and first heard many of these ideas in raw form—especially our community group and my women's Bible study table 2015–2016.

These counseling colleagues past and present have provided not only professional but also personal camaraderie and courage in the battle against shame, including reading and/or discussing portions of this book: Ryan Davidson, Penny Freeman, Wendy King, Melissa Moore, and Belinda Pendleton.

Thank you to my fellow writer-warriors, Heidi Carlson, Lauren Washer, and Mary Yonkman, whose real-life writings, blogging, and friendships spur me on to the same. Hannah Anderson, Christina Fox, Gloria Furman, Jen Michel, and Jen Wilkin pioneered the way for me and cheered me along to "dare greatly" from the time we first met through The Gospel Coalition.

None of this would have happened had not Crossway been willing to take on a new writer. Thanks to James Kinnard's introduction to Dave DeWit, whose careful editing and supportive coaching throughout this process have been invaluable. I have enjoyed working with every member of Crossway's team, with special shout-outs to the cover design team and the marketing team under Amy Kruis's leadership. Tara Davis, my copy editor extraordinaire, edited with care, precision, and gentleness—all that a first-time author could hope for!

I would not have embarked on such a venture without the wholehearted support of my husband, Seth, and the many sacrifices he made to free me to engage in the writing process. Lucia and Alethia, thanks for letting Mommy write and for reminding me how to dance, play, and create as you do so shamelessly and effortlessly.

Above all else, I thank God, who is the Author of my story, and in whose Son Jesus Christ we have hope of being unashamed. He is the reason I write, now and always.

Most of the examples used throughout this book are a combination of various characteristics of friends, clients, and/or my own life. Proper permission has been sought and granted for the few examples that are not composites, and in all cases, identifying names and details have been changed to protect anonymity and privacy.

This book is not intended to be a substitute for the advice of a professional counselor or a licensed physician. Readers should consult with their counselors and/or doctors in any matters relating to their health.

Introduction

Shame: Everyone Has It

I have always been terrified of public speaking. I can trace it back to eighth-grade graduation, when I froze on stage in front of my classmates and an audience of hundreds. Standing in front of the mic unable to utter a word, the expectant and anxious waiting, and an uncomfortable and heavy silence—these are what I fear anytime I am about to take the podium. This fear of being publicly embarrassed, of my weakness being unmasked in front of an audience who sees each excruciating moment, is one manifestation of shame in my life. At its core, shame is fear of weakness, failure, or unworthiness being unveiled for all to see, or fear that at least one other person will notice that which we want to hide. Shame is like a chameleon, easily blending into the surrounding environment so that it can't directly be seen.

Shame commonly masquerades as embarrassment, or the nagging sense of "not quite good enough." It shows up when you attempt a new venture, or when you're unsure of your place in a group. Unchecked, it can become an impenetrable barrier between you and others. It is not a topic of conversation at a party, although it is an unwelcome guest in every gathering. You may not know if you suffer under shame, because too often it's been categorized as guilt (which is its close cousin). It is not the exclusive domain of victims of abuse, yet shame is found in every story of suffering at the hands of another. Shame can linger when you have sinned against another in ways that feel unforgiveable. Shame is complicated.

Perhaps it might help to consider a few scenarios where shame begins to show itself.

Monique and Tony walk into a party full of laughing, well-dressed people, and Monique inwardly freezes. She is back in the halls of her high school, where she was always on the outside of such groups. She cannot bear to replay the story of rejection, and she wants to turn around and leave before they are noticed. It would be safer to go home.

Blake confesses his sexual addiction to Emily, and tears run down her cheeks. How could he? Emily berates him with all that she is feeling in that moment. Then she turns cold for weeks, barely speaking to him while cocooned within her books, journals, and work. She is alone, and so is he.

Christie's voice is hoarse from screaming at her toddlers. She glances at the windows, thankful they're closed and the neighbors can't hear the angry tirade that would discredit her as the kind, good Christian they think she is. She feels furious most of all with herself for losing it, and she does not know if she can find her way back to grace this time. Surely there are limits to God's forgiveness of an angry mom?

Sam's red-rimmed eyes betray the late night at the bar the evening prior. He could not bear to hear Kelly's relentless criticism, and so he found refuge in the only place that felt safe. He feels like he can never be weak in front of her. His only option is to leave her presence and regroup until he can be the strong man she expects him to be for her.[1]

Anna weeps over the phone with her best friend as she describes a marriage that feels hopeless and lifeless. No matter what she tries, Will cannot seem to see her, care about her, or change the behavior that is destroying their marriage and their family. She tells no one, for fear of what others would say—a dismissal or an attempt to minimize the pain she lives with daily.

Jake is alone. He assumed that by age thirty he would be well on his way to his dream of a successful career, marriage, and starting a family. Instead, Jake works an unmotivating job and cannot seem to garner enough courage to talk to the women he admires from afar, much less to ask them on a date. The worst day for him? Sundays, because he sits in a pew by himself surrounded by those who seem to have what he's missing. But what is he missing? Why can't he ever shake the feeling of "not quite good enough"?

Laura walked into fourth grade acutely aware of the new item she wore. She could finally read the blackboard without squinting, thanks to her first pair of glasses. The plastic pink frames were the object of much attention from her fellow students, and it wasn't long before she heard the name: "Four Eyes!" From that moment, she counted the years until her eye doctor would permit her to be fitted for contacts. It would be eighth grade.

~

All of these scenarios describe shame. It's a word we do not often use in daily conversation, book groups, or church pulpits, but shame is something we all experience. It's the feeling that we have missed the mark according to our own standard or our perception of someone else's standard for us. Shame keeps us from being honest about our struggles, sins, and less-than-perfect moments. Fear of shame drives us to perfectionism in all areas of our lives, so that there would be no imperfection to be noticed and judged.[2] Shame is what we heap on others when they fail us. Shame keeps us holding onto bitterness and refusing to forgive. We are impacted by the shame of sin committed against us, and this drives a wedge into our relationships.

Shame can be darker and deeper too. It's what a perpetrator gives to his victim as he violates her. She will carry that shame forever unless she can find a way to bring it into the light of day. To disown it, she needs to name the shame as his. Shame can be the lack of parental affection and attention that leaves a child with the indelible mark of "not worthy." Shame arises from past sin that seems to forever haunt you. You know, *that* sin that you feel like you can't share with anyone.

So you stay in hiding, holed up in your lonely bunker of one, never letting anyone get close enough to see you, to see *that* part of you.

"Shame is the intensely painful feeling or experience of believing that we are flawed and therefore unworthy of love and belonging," writes Brené Brown.[3] Throughout this book, I will refer often to Brown's research and findings. So you might wonder, why read this book instead of hers? I want to put her work into a biblical framework that will help make sense of life in a fallen world. If you're not a Christian and you're reading this book, I would ask you to have a bit of patience and keep reading. You'll find that the topic of shame is worth addressing with hope. I believe that you will benefit greatly from the discussion from asking yourself: In what (or whom) do I hope?

Shame and Guilt: Similar, but Different

How is shame different from guilt? It's crucial to understand the distinction. Brown writes: "The majority of shame researchers and clinicians agree that the difference between shame and guilt is best understood as the difference between 'I am bad' and 'I did something bad.' Guilt = I did something bad. Shame = I am bad."[4] Guilt is associated with actions while shame taints your entire identity. Ed Welch, a professor and counselor at the Christian Counseling and Educational Foundation (CCEF), fills this out in the following ways:

- "Guilt can be hidden; shame feels like it is always exposed."[5]

- "Guilt lives in the courtroom where you stand alone before the judge. It says, 'You are responsible for wrongdoing. . . . You are wrong. . . . You have sinned.' *The guilty person expects punishment and needs forgiveness.*"[6]
- "Shame lives in the community, though the community can feel like a courtroom. It says, 'You don't belong—you are unacceptable, unclean, and disgraced' because 'You are wrong, you have sinned' *or* 'Wrong has been done to you' *or* 'You are associated with those who are disgraced or outcast.' The shamed person *feels worthless, expects rejection, and needs cleansing, fellowship [community], love, and acceptance.*"[7]

To expunge guilt, confession and forgiveness are needed. Eradicating shame calls for a deep and pervasive antidote, one that will strike shame at its root and transform the way you think about who you are and the relationships in your life. Brown begins to touch on this when she says, "The antidote to shame is empathy and vulnerability."[8] Many relationships have been transformed by putting into practice increased empathetic responses and vulnerable sharing. Conflicts often arise because one person struggles with vulnerability (closes off/shuts down/withdraws) and the other has a hard time with empathy (does not listen without judging in order to understand, or does not listen at all). It is easy to see how a lack of empathy leads to a diminishing vulnerability, which leads to a lack of empathy, and on and on it goes. Interrupting this cycle is crucial. But we know that our ability to empathize and be vulnerable is not enough to heal shame at its source.

The Limits of Empathy and Vulnerability

Most of us can think of a time when we risked vulnerability only to experience deeper rejection, and therefore our shame messages were reinforced. And most of us can likewise think about how being empathetic was not enough to encourage the deceptive spouse or betrayed friend to trust us again or to tell the truth. There must be more than empathy and vulnerability. We live in world of broken people who cannot at the end of the day be trusted with our most vulnerable selves, nor can they trust us to be as empathetic as needed when they are in their most fragile moments. We all have been disappointed by others, and we all have disappointed friends, family, colleagues, and spouses—even those with whom we claim deepest intimacy. We wear shame like a shield, hiding who we know ourselves to be and protecting ourselves from whom we fear others could be.

Into the dark hopelessness of the human condition steps a Person—one who left his perfect relationship of impeccable empathy and total vulnerability; who left the perfect place where neither guilt nor shame exists because sin is absent; and who chose to leave perfect trust to be utterly vulnerable. He who knew the depths of the darkness of human hearts entrusted himself to us as a baby, making himself so vulnerable that he would not physically survive without human care. He who had never felt betrayal was betrayed by his closest friends, and he who knew no sin *became sin for us*, feeling to the depths of his being our pain. There is no greater empathy than how Isaiah describes Jesus: "Surely he has borne our griefs and carried our sorrows" (Isa. 53:4). It is in relationship with this grief-laden Savior that our shame will begin to dissipate. It is through his vulnerability that we learn to entrust ourselves to fellow broken people, and it is in his empathy that we know we are never alone, though all humans may betray or disappoint us.

Through union with Christ you are clothed with honor rather than shame, made part of a community to which you will always belong, and given a kingdom that cannot be taken away. Walking by faith according to our true identity of being "hidden with Christ in God" (Col. 3:3) will transform our relationships, our parenting, our churches, our marriages, and our work. Shame will linger for as long as we await the life to come, but its voice will become quieter and its claims less insistent as we remember the reality that its hold on us is limited and fleeting.

For Reflection and Discussion

1. How would you define shame? How is it different from guilt?
2. Which shame scenario do you identify with the most?
3. When has someone disappointed you? Can you think of a time when you disappointed someone else?
4. How is Jesus an embodiment of perfect empathy and vulnerability?

1

Exchanging Shame for Beauty

And I will deal severely with all who have
    oppressed you.
  I will save the weak and helpless ones;
I will bring together
    those who were chased away.
I will give glory and fame to my former exiles,
    wherever they have been mocked and shamed.

Zephaniah 3:19 (NLT)

One glance at your clothing, and I tend to make assumptions about who you are, what you do, perhaps even where you live. Why is clothing so defining? Clothes indicate purpose, even employment. When you're in aisle six at Target looking for your kid's favorite brand of cereal, you probably look for that familiar red shirt indicating an employee. Clothing serves to identify us.

Shame can clothe you or expose you. It comes after struggling yet again with the bad habit you're trying to break, or the temptation you've given in to after days of resistance. It's what I feel like I'm wearing when I have yelled at my children (again). I go back and ask them to forgive me, but shame is that lingering sense that I have failed beyond rescue. That I have failed because *I am a failure*. Shame clothes me because I have not met my own expectations, nor those of my culture. In our Western American culture, male anger is usually tolerated more than female anger. So when I as a woman erupt in anger, my shame increases because I am not supposed to struggle with *this* type of sin.

I know that the *guilt* of my sin is covered because I believe the Bible's promises, such as what we find in Romans 6:23: "For the wages of sin is death, but the free gift of God is eternal life in Christ Jesus our Lord," and Psalm 32:5: "I acknowledged my sin to you, and did not cover up my iniquity. I said, 'I will confess my transgressions to the LORD.' And you forgave the iniquity of my sin," but how do I get rid of the *shame*?

Shame clothes me when my failure has been noticed by another. For instance, if I get condescending, judgmental, or pitying looks from fellow shoppers in the midst of my child's tantrum, I feel cloaked in the shame of being judged as a bad mom. If I give a public presentation that doesn't go well, I feel ashamed because I failed with an audience.

Shame is cyclical. Sometimes we feel shamed by another's

behavior toward us, and we try to get rid of the shame by giving it to someone else. The problem is that shame cannot be transferred. It multiplies like yeast in a batch of rising dough. My husband shamed me/us through nodding off while talking to dinner guests, and I felt like he betrayed my standard of perfect hospitality. Therefore I returned the shame to him through a demeaning comment about him in front of our guests. Where does shame stop? How can we break the cycle of reacting to shame with more shame? We have to change our clothes, our identities. We need new clothing, and when exposed by shame, we need adequate clothing.

A Biblical History of Clothing

Our first parents discovered the problem of inadequate clothing the hard way in the garden of Eden at the beginning of time. In Genesis 3, we see Adam and Eve hiding from God, because after sinning by eating the forbidden fruit, they realized they were naked. Their first impulse was to sew fig leaves together to make clothes (v. 7). Of course, these clothes were not enough to cover their guilt and the resulting shame from knowing their relationship with God was broken. And so even while clothed, they hid from God as he walked toward them (v. 8). After their confrontation, which is full of questions on God's part and blame-shifting by Adam and Eve, God pronounces the curse—declaring the brokenness that would seep into all of humanity and creation because of their rebellion. They are expelled from Eden, and the chapter ends.

But before the bleak ending of Genesis 3, there is an act of mercy and love we often overlook. "And the LORD God made for Adam and for his wife garments of skins and clothed them" (v. 21). He who remembers that we are dust knows that the fig-leaf loincloths will not cover them sufficiently, so he does what they cannot do for themselves: *he clothes them.* The clothing required death of animals, and here we see the first sacrifice. Although it might seem like an unnecessary sacrifice because it did not atone for their sin (a Redeemer would have to come for that), it *did* cover their shame—at least temporarily.

Does your clothing do that for you?

In the very beginning of creation, at the point of sin's entrance into an otherwise perfect Paradise, clothing comes both as a result of sin and as covering for the shame sin always brings in its wake. Adam and Eve need clothing because sin has opened their eyes to their nakedness; but God gives clothing because his eyes are opened with compassion to the shame that now exists in them because of sin.

Clothing covers, and it identifies. Only clothing given by God can do anything about the shame you and I wear as a garment, or the shame that we feel we cannot escape because it perpetually unclothes us. We see echoes of this theme throughout redemptive history as it unfolds in the pages of the Old Testament. Those without clothing are marked by shame, and those with shame are marked by their clothing. The story of Tamar illustrates this tragically. She is raped by her brother Amnon who immediately despises her after he has violated her: "Then Amnon hated her with very great hatred, so that the hatred with which he hated her was greater than the love with which he had loved her" (2 Sam. 13:15). He calls his servant to put her out of his house, and the scene of what happens to her clothing is painted vividly:

> Now she was wearing a long robe with sleeves, for thus were the virgin daughters of the king dressed. So his servant put her out and bolted the door after her. And Tamar put ashes on her head and tore the long robe that she wore. And she laid her hand on her head and went away, crying aloud as she went. (2 Sam. 13:18–19)

We find few scenes in the Bible more tragic than this one. God is moved to compassion for this woman in her shame because of sin committed against her, violation of the most tragic kind. He sees her shame vividly, even when her own father, King David, ignores it and minimizes it. God does not retaliate by giving violence back for violence as her brother Absalom tries to do (and subsequently throws the entire kingdom into an uproar). Instead, he promises a Redeemer who will be a perfect King and perfect defender. He hears, and he answers the question Tamar asks that falls on the deaf ears of her lust-filled brother: "As for me, where could I carry my shame?" (2 Sam. 13:13). This One will be moved to compassion by those like Tamar, we who wear the ashes of shame like a garment. He will carry her shame and ours to its full extent, with arms stretched wide on a beam of wood. Tamar was forced to wait for the perfect king to do what David could not do: bring the justice she longed for and restore the dignity Amnon stole from her. In Jesus, we now have the perfect King, who promises his people, "Then you will know that I am the LORD; those who wait for me shall not be put to shame" (Isa. 49:23).

Isaiah records Jesus's mission statement this way:

> The Spirit of the Lord GOD is upon me,
>> because the LORD has anointed me
> to bring good news to the poor;
>> he has sent me to bind up the brokenhearted,
> to proclaim liberty to the captives,
>> and the opening of the prison to those who are
>>> bound;
> to proclaim the year of the LORD's favor,
>> and the day of vengeance of our God;
>> to comfort all who mourn;
> to grant to those who mourn in Zion—
>> *to give them a beautiful headdress instead of ashes,*
> *the oil of gladness instead of mourning,*
>> *the garment of praise instead of a faint spirit;*
> that they may be called oaks of righteousness,
>> the planting of the LORD, that he may be glorified. . . .
> Instead of your shame there shall be a double portion;
>> instead of dishonor they shall rejoice in their lot;
> therefore in their land they shall possess a double
>> portion;
>> they shall have everlasting joy." (Isa. 61:1–3, 7)

Garments of Joy, Beauty, and Honor

No one who feels shame experiences true joy. A client once told me that it had been years since she was happy, and in the next breath said that she constantly felt shame. She could never shake the feeling of not measuring up, the feeling that God was angry with her. Although she knew the truth intellectually, she told me in tears, "I want to be free!"

Joy is a hallmark of one who is free from shame. Jesus comes to bring joy as he removes your garments of shame and gives you a royal headdress instead. In place of shame, he gives honor, beauty, joy, comfort, justice, favor, and freedom—what our hearts long for most when shame rules our emotions, thoughts, and desires.

We actually crave these *more* than empathy and vulnerability, which Brené Brown prescribes as shame's antidote. Practicing empathy and vulnerability is a start. They point you down a path of acknowledging how pervasive shame is to the human experience, but they offer no permanent remedy.

What about a holistic cure that reaches each aspect of shame's damage? Consider what Jesus offers:

- Jesus comes to give honor instead of dishonor—all the ways you have felt and experienced rejection.
- Jesus clothes you with beauty, removing the ashes of shame you've worn for your sin or for the sinful atrocities committed against you.
- He comforts you as you mourn, releasing you from the shame of grieving alone or without purpose.
- Whether in this life or in the one to come, he brings justice for the injustice you've suffered because of your race, faith, gender, or family.
- Jesus brings favor—oh, favor of the Lord that is permanent and unchanging—instead of the vague cloud of constant disapproval.

And what is the result of Christ's work? Joy and freedom, the exact opposite of shame. Shame always steals joy and limits freedom. Shame binds us in chains that feel unbreakable to realities that seem unchangeable. Jesus frees you in the Spirit of the Lord.

The Great Shame Exchange

How can Jesus free you from shame? Through something as simple and as hard as faith. It is a faith that agrees that you cannot rescue yourself from your shame, that your attempts to clothe yourself have been as futile as the fig-leaf loincloths our first parents crafted. It is a faith that addresses the complication of shame mingled with guilt. This faith gives you an underlying confidence that your sin truly has been atoned for and taken away by a dying-now-resurrected Savior. It's a faith that puts you at the mercy of the only trustworthy One, realizing that his human image-bearers have failed you in a myriad of ways, and that you have also failed those around you. It is a faith filled with hope that freedom is possible *because it is promised by this trustworthy One*, guaranteed by the signature of a promise signed with his own blood.

This shame exchange is costly. Jesus willingly clothed himself with your dishonor, giving his shame-free identity to you if you will be united to him in faith. It is very costly for Christ, but not for us. All it costs us is the humility of admitting we cannot cover our own shame. We receive honor; he took our shame. We are lavished with grace; he was stained with our sin. We receive salvation; he experienced damnation. Because

Jesus was separated from the Father, we never will have to be. "Indeed, *none* who wait for you [God] shall be put to shame" (Ps. 25:3). "None" except for one, Jesus Christ, who bore our sin, guilt, and shame, that we might know forgiveness, redemption, and freedom.

If you are wondering how to begin the shame exchange, try to pray along with these cries of the psalmist:

- "O my God, in you I trust; let me not be put to shame; let not my enemies exult over me" (Ps. 25:2).
- "Oh, guard my soul, and deliver me! Let me not be put to shame, for I take refuge in you" (Ps. 25:20).
- "In you, O LORD, do I take refuge; let me never be put to shame; in your righteousness deliver me!" (Ps. 31:1).
- "O LORD, let me not be put to shame, for I call upon you" (Ps. 31:17).
- "You know my reproach, and my shame and my dishonor; my foes are all known to you" (Ps. 69:1).
- "Uphold me according to your promise, that I may live, and let me not be put to shame in my hope!" (Ps. 119:116).

As you pray and cry out to this Lord, asking him that you would not be put to shame, remember that you pray with the cross and resurrection in the rearview mirror—a signature guaranteeing the certainty that we are heard and we will be answered. Shame is often tied to the past. We ruminate about past failures or sins, or past abuses we suffered, or words spoken to us in formative stages of life that seem to lodge forever in our heart's memory. We who dwell in shame must remember that shame's remedy is also past. "It is finished," Jesus cried from the cross, and that cry echoes into every corner of sin and shame and brokenness (John 19:30). We can know that what was finished on the cross will be fully realized at the end of days. Instead of living enchained to past shame, we can live tethered to future hope of our shame-free destiny. We will be clothed in wedding garments of "white linen, bright and pure" (Rev. 19:8).There will be no shame in the dwelling place of God, which our clothing will serve to reflect.

Where We Are Going: Shame Disappears in Community

Because we are clothed with Christ's perfect honor, we can put off shame's ragged lies now. I am no longer a shamed one; I am an honored one. And so are you. So how do we live in the present when shame raises its ugly head?

We must recognize that we are not alone. Shame cannot stand the light of community and truth-telling. As I sat with two friends at Starbucks one Saturday afternoon, I felt our shame melt away as we shared our eerily similar middle school shame stories, which had been triggered by present-day situations. I shared about the way that all the girls in my eighth-grade class decided that they did not like me. To feel and experience my peers' rejection at the age of thirteen deeply branded me with shame that has not been easily overcome. I feel it each time I come to a new group. Will they accept me? How long before the group turns against me? Shame tells me that I am unworthy and there is something deeply repulsive about who I am.

My friends joined in with their own stories. One shared

about a list the girls in her middle school wrote about her, delineating all of the reasons they no longer liked her. We each described almost obsessive desires to include others so that no would ever feel rejected like we had felt. We are all recovering people-pleasers learning not to fear rejection and to speak up when truth needs to be shared in the context of our jobs and relationships. Many days we live confident of our unshakeable identities in Jesus, honored instead of defined by the past experience of rejection. We are committed to being part of our Redeemer's shame-eradication mission in each other's lives. We know that we can go to each other, share the shame we're feeling, and be met with empathy *and a reminder of our gospel identity*.

Your sin is forgiven, yes and amen, and how we need this daily! But Jesus came to do even more than give you a blank slate. In union with Christ by faith, honor is part of your past and your future. Beauty rather than ashes, joy instead of despair. You are a new person—not merely an "ex-sinner" but a redeemed saint. Do you doubt this?

Think about Paul's addresses to the churches in the New Testament. If the apostle Paul were writing your church a letter, it probably would not be a letter of commendation. The usual pattern in the Epistles is that there is egregious sin that must be confronted (e.g., the Corinthian church that was tolerating a number of sexual sins, as well as drunkenness at the Lord's Supper) and poor theology that needs to be corrected (e.g., the Thessalonian church that had stopped engaging in their daily work life because they were sitting around waiting for heaven).

Poor theology always leads to sinful practice, and sinful living is always rooted in poor theology—misunderstanding and misbelieving who God is, what the Bible teaches, and who Christians are. Yet despite the brokenness of the churches to which Paul writes (reminding us that there has *never* been a perfect church nor will there be), he begins almost every letter the same way. See if you can detect the pattern:

- "To all those in Rome who are loved by God and called to be saints" (Rom. 1:7).
- "To the church of God that is in Corinth, to those who are sanctified in Christ Jesus, called to be saints together with all those who call upon the name of our Lord Jesus Christ, both their Lord and ours" (1 Cor. 1:2).
- "To the church of God that is at Corinth, with all the saints who are in the whole of Achaia" (2 Cor. 1:1).
- "To the saints who are in Ephesus, and are faithful in Christ Jesus" (Eph. 1:1).
- "To all the saints in Christ Jesus who are at Philippi" (Phil. 1:1).
- "To the saints and faithful brothers in Christ at Colossae" (Col. 1:2).

Do you see it? Paul addresses them all as *saints*. Saints are those who are holy, set apart, and linked with God's holiness. And if you believe in Jesus, *this is who you already are*. Remembering and meditating on your identity *within the community of fellow saints* will help to weaken shame's hold on your life.

We must see how your story of shame and my story of

shame connect to the story of Christ's covering our shame. Jesus is the only true refuge for the shame-filled; he came to clothe every area of your life with his honor and righteousness.

In my journey of shame, which started in the middle-school classroom, having traveling companions has made all the difference. They help me to press deeper into the truth that is always ready to be rediscovered. I am clothed in honor and beauty instead of shame. Instead of my exclusion, Jesus was placed "outside the camp" so that I might be brought in to the fellowship of the Divine. Jesus experienced separation from God the Father so that I would never be rejected from the one whose acceptance matters eternally. Instead of feeling quieted by shame, I am learning to speak up as an honored, beloved daughter of the King of kings within the community to which I belong—right beside you as you do the same.

Will you join me as I examine major types of shame—body shame, performance shame, and relationship shame—and the various arenas where our shame threatens to hijack our lives, including parenting, marriage, and church? Will you dare to look at the places in your life that are tainted with shame and bring them into the light of Jesus's life, death, and resurrection for you? Will you suspend your doubts and perhaps even your cynicism for a few pages and find an honor waiting for you that answers your deepest feelings of unworthiness?

For Reflection and Discussion

1. What makes you feel exposed to shame? How have you tried to cover it?

2. How does God offer to clothe your shame? How do you know you can trust him to do so?
3. What difference would it make for you to view yourself as a saint?
4. What is one small step of faith you could take to begin to be rescued from your shame?

2

Living Shamelessly through Christ-Formed Community

Christian community is not an ideal we have to realize, but rather a reality created by God in Christ
in which we may participate. The more clearly we
learn to recognize that the ground and strength and
promise of all our community is in Jesus Christ
alone, the more calmly we will learn to think about
our community and pray and hope for it.

Dietrich Bonhoeffer

Every time she visits, I feel it. I am not quite good enough.
My house is not clean enough. I am acutely aware of the toy
minefield this friend has to walk through to make it from the
front door into the living room. One time after she left, my

husband, Seth, arrived home to find me furiously vacuuming our rugs. I told him with a cynical laugh, "I am vacuuming up my shame!" I could blame her for my shame. I could say that she is a "shaming person," one whose presence emits that feeling of judgment. Yet Seth never feels like this when she visits. Ever. And if asked, I imagine that she would not agree with my assessment. So what is the problem?

It's Not You, It's Me

I can think of a few problems. One is that I battle between "ideal me" and "real me." Ideal me is a good Southern housewife/successful professional/creative-yet-organized mom who engages my children while keeping the household running smoothly and working as a counselor/writer/event speaker. Real me maybe can do one of those things well in any given day or week. Inevitably the house settles into a less-than-clean state, and the evidence of our work and play remains in full display. This is all normal, my fellow moms-in-the-trenches assure me. Yet I can't seem to shake the feeling of worthlessness when I see our home in disarray, a far cry from the homes pictured on the glossy magazines peeking out from under the piles of dirty socks and discarded toys on our coffee table.

The real problem with the well-meaning friend's visit is that she serves to expose my own self-doubts and an identity too closely tied to others' perceived opinions of me. I am hardwired to pick up on external shame because I feel like I deserve it. And yet I cannot talk myself into truth. I treasure amazing promises like Galatians 5:1: "It is for freedom that Christ has set you free. Therefore, stand firm, and do not be yoked again to a yoke of slavery." Colossians 3 reminds me that my true life is hidden with Christ in God, that my destiny is glory, that I am part of God's "chosen ones, holy and beloved." Ephesians proclaims that through faith in Jesus Christ I am showered with "the immeasurable riches of his grace" and that I am the object of "the love of Christ that surpasses knowledge" in order to be "filled with all the fullness of God." So why should a crumb-littered rug matter in light of such radiant promises?

Community as Essential to Christ's Shame-Redemption Plan

I have a belief problem, and this belief problem cannot disappear in solitude. As humans made in God's image, we are created for relationship. It was not good for Adam to be alone, and so Eve was formed. When God called Abraham into a faith relationship with him, the purpose was for all nations to be blessed; this would happen through a people group set apart to exhibit God's faithfulness through their community. When God calls us into relationship with himself, he joins us to a community.

Not surprisingly, recent findings in neuroscience confirm these truths. Brené Brown summarizes one researcher as follows: "In his book *Social Intelligence: The New Science of Human Relationships,* Daniel Goleman explores how the latest findings in biology and neuroscience confirm that we are hardwired for connection and that our relationships shape our biology as well as our experiences. Goleman writes, 'Even our most routine encounters act as regulators in the brain, priming our emotions, some desirable, others not. The more strongly connected we are with someone emotionally, the greater the mutual force.' It's amazing—yet perhaps not surprising—that the connectedness we experience in our relationships impacts the way our brain develops and performs."[1]

The biblical term for "connection" is *community*. When Jesus came to earth, he entered as part of a family and then gathered twelve disciples around him when he started his public ministry. He is rarely seen apart from community. In addition to the disciples, we read in the Gospels of significant relationships with Mary, Martha, Lazarus, Mary Magdalene, "the tax collectors and sinners," Nicodemas, and Zaccheus. Jesus is almost always seen relating to people—whether healing their diseases, confronting their distorted beliefs about God, or proclaiming the kingdom of God to the multitudes.

One of the most damaging ideas in recent Christian theology is that it is holier to be in solitude than to be in community. While it is certainly true that there are necessary seasons of prayer, fasting, and individual study of Scripture in the life of a Christian, these are to be seen as missional (meaning, they are to strengthen and equip us to be sent out into community and relationship). Great harm occurs when we divorce our private devotional lives from our relationships. First John 3:20–21 speaks to this: "If anyone says, 'I love God,' and hates his brother, he is a liar; for he who does not love his brother whom he has seen cannot love God whom he has not seen. And this commandment we have from him: whoever loves God must also love his brother." James, Jesus's brother, states it even more strongly:

> But be doers of the word, and not hearers only, deceiving yourselves. For if anyone is a hearer of the word and not a doer, he is like a man who looks intently at his natural face in a mirror. For he looks at himself and goes away and at once forgets what he was like. But the one who looks into the perfect law, the law of liberty, and perseveres, being no hearer who forgets but a doer who acts, he will be blessed in his doing. (James 1:22–25)

To be in relationship with God by faith requires expression through relationships of love. All of the Epistles connect teaching about who we are as Christians with exhortations about how to love others. Each action of love fueled by faith, regardless of how hidden, small, or imperfect, is helping to build communities where every member is honored and finds a place to belong.

So what does this have to do with shame? Christ came to clothe our shame with honor, and he has made us part of communities that are called to be visible, physical reflections of this replacing of shame with esteem and respect (honor). Imagine belonging to a community characterized by the following:

- Genuine love that seeks the best for the other
- Empathy that experiences both the joys and sorrows of life together as if it were your own
- Honoring one another's dignity regardless of job, socioeconomic status, personality type, or family background

- Guaranteed forgiveness for every wrong instead of retribution
- Each member committed to being peaceable

It may sound too good to be true. Yet it's taken directly from the pages of the Bible, part of many instructions to God's people on how to relate to one another (Rom. 12:9–18).

Meeting Shame with the Grace of Forgiveness

The Bible is unique in its approach to community because it holds in tension both the ideal vision of people living in harmony with one another and the reality that our sin and brokenness will often disrupt this harmony. It allows for repair of the inevitable fissures that happen as we try to love one another perfectly with hearts that are imperfect. Recently I told my husband, "I'm really good at ruining relationships." I said this after a particularly trying week where my agenda had been crossed (mostly by my family), and I had lashed out in criticism and anger toward those I love the most. I felt discouraged and hypocritical, particularly since I was writing a chapter about shame being healed through redemptive community. His quick reply cut me to the heart, giving me grace and hope amidst the shame I felt about my sin: "But you're also really good at repairing relationships."

Therein lies your hope, too. For you will break relationships and be broken by those you love. Yet God offers restoration to you and for you with others. God writes our inevitable failings into his prescription for redemptive community, and he teaches us what it means to forgive. Scripture provides his instruction:

- "[Forgive your brother or sister who sins against you] not seven times, but seventy-seven times" (Matt. 18:22).
- "Be kind to one another, tenderhearted, forgiving one another, as God in Christ forgave you" (Eph. 4:32).
- "Put on then, as God's chosen ones, holy and beloved, compassionate hearts, kindness, humility, meekness, and patience, bearing with one another and, if one has a complaint against another, forgiving each other; as the Lord has forgiven you, so you also must forgive" (Col. 3:12–13).

Living in the reality of God's forgiveness of us requires a posture of forgiveness toward others. And when we receive forgiveness from others, it makes us grateful for God's forgiveness of us, and the cycle of redemption rolls along like the reassuring tide of the ocean's waves. Shame tends to resist accepting forgiveness. It wants to think it needs to be earned, or that it has never done quite enough, or that the mistakes or sin or imperfection are too pervasive for forgiveness; therefore, I'm not worthy.

This is part of why we are called to practice forgiveness in community. For you need my forgiveness as much as I will need yours. You will need me to show grace by overlooking a wrong (Prov. 19:11), and I will need you to do the same. Together we are called to radically oppose shame's lies by relating to one another from an attitude of grace and forgiveness. Many times this may be as simple (and counterintuitive) as staying in a difficult family relationship, friendship, small group, or church instead of fleeing at the first sign of failure and weakness. It is gracious to give space to our fellow strugglers. As an example, almost every parent and adult child who are still in relationship beyond adolescence are evidence of the power of forgiveness and the shame-healing work of loving another through multiple years and seasons. (Or perhaps I'm just thinking of my own parents and their time-tested patience with me and both of my brothers!)

As I wrestled with the feeling of exposure and lingering shame that I could not vacuum up because of my less-than-clean house, I reached out to a trusted friend and asked for her input. For times such as this, when you're feeling your most vulnerable, it is important to have identified someone who is "safe" to confide in. Safe does not mean perfect (since none of us are *that*). A safe confidant is someone who has proven over time his or her commitment to you, someone you can trust to be both honest and gentle with you and who allows you to similarly speak into his or her life. Such friends give you space for your feelings and thoughts, and they share theirs with you, too. Psychologists Henry Cloud and John Townsend define safe people as those who are characterized primarily by three characteristics: (1) the ability to connect with us through being emotionally present with us; (2) a posture of gracious acceptance toward us; and (3) authenticity and mutual sharing of truth with us.[2]

In my case, my confidant encouraged me with this truth: "It sounds like the only one holding you captive is yourself." She shared this after empathizing with my frustration and laughing with me about the concept of vacuuming up shame from the toy-littered floors that are all too familiar to both of us. As I walked away from this conversation, I felt freer and lighter.

The promise of Christ's freedom from Galatians 5:1 had put on flesh and spoken words of truth to me in the context of love.

Community Shame-Resisting Practices

As part of the community we belong to through Jesus Christ, we are called to invite others into this community and to foster the sense of belonging that we are given by God through Jesus Christ. Ray Ortlund, a senior pastor with decades of ministry experience, describes this type of community when he writes about the church:

> The family of God is where people behave in a new way. I think of it with a simple equation: gospel + safety + time. The family of God is where people should find lots of gospel, lots of safety, and lots of time. In other words, the people in our churches need:
>
> - multiple exposures to the happy news of the gospel from one end of the Bible to the other;
> - the safety of non-accusing sympathy so that they can admit their problems honestly; and
> - enough time to rethink their lives at a deep level, because people are complex and changing is not easy.
>
> In a gentle church like this, no one is put under pressure or singled out for embarrassment. Everyone is free to open up, and we all grow together as we look to Jesus.[3]

The church community Ortlund describes is a result of living out the multiple "one another" commands given throughout the New Testament. Consider a few of them:

- Love one another (John 13:34; 1 Pet. 1:22; 1 John 3:11, 23; 4:7, 11–12; 2 John 1:5).
- Clothe yourselves with humility toward one another (1 Pet. 5:5).
- Stop passing judgment on one another (Rom. 14:13).
- Accept one another (Rom. 15:7).
- Encourage one another and build each other up (1 Thess. 5:11; Heb. 3:13; 10:25).
- Do not slander one another (James 4:11).
- Speak the truth to one another (Eph. 4:25; Col. 3:8–9).
- Don't grumble against one another (James 5:9).
- Confess your sins to one another (James 5:16).
- Offer hospitality to one another (Rom. 12:13; Heb. 13:1–2; 1 Pet. 4:9).
- Serve one another (Gal. 5:13; 1 Pet. 4:10).
- Comfort one another (1 Thess. 4:18; 5:14).
- Be kind and compassionate to one another (Eph. 4:32).

All of these "one another" commands are given to express who God has created us to be in Jesus Christ, and they are a reflection of how God treats us in Jesus. Imagine how the practice of these life-giving commands could transform your home, your neighborhood, your church, your community, your city, your workplace!

The Importance of Welcome

Let's take one command from this list and explore it further: "Offer hospitality to one another without grumbling" (1 Pet. 4:9, NIV). *Hospitality* is defined as "the friendly and generous reception and entertainment of guests, visitors, or strangers."[4]

Another definition adds: "The quality or disposition of receiving and treating guests and strangers in a warm, friendly, generous way."[5]

I will never forget the way that Mexican families welcomed our group of American college students into their homes the summer I spent in Guadalajara. We were strangers—bumbling about with their beautiful language and fumbling cultural customs left and right—and they welcomed us to their family dinner tables. They served us their best food and gave us generous love that we could feel despite the language barrier. Latin American culture is known for its hospitality toward strangers, and every experience that summer served to confirm that reputation.

What might it look like if we extended similar welcome to our next-door neighbors and new friends we meet as well as to the immigrants and strangers in our midst? How could this begin to dispel the shame inherent in our Western American culture of being different—of feeling like an outsider? Consider the last time you were welcomed into another's home, office, play group, or party. What did your host or hostess do to help you feel comfortable? Did they pour you a drink? Or take your coat? Or engage you in conversation? Or introduce you to others? There are a thousand ways we can offer hospitality to others, and it begins with overcoming your own shame that would tell you you're not worthy of another's time or attention.

God is a welcoming, inviting God who is constantly reaching out to his people. He is a God who makes himself known and begins with a greeting. The first sign of shame is that Adam and Eve hid from God's daily welcome. The first sign of redemptive grace is that God still called out to them. He has continued to do so throughout the centuries of relationship with people who run from him, attempt to hide from him, or cover themselves because of shame in his presence. He welcomes his people, and we are to do the same.

Offering hospitality to others—whether it be through inviting them into your home or to meet you for coffee or lunch—requires some measure of risk-taking. They may reject your invitation for reasons of their own (perhaps shame?). Practicing welcome will force us to live contrary to the shame stories that become our default setting, communicating that not only is the friend/stranger/visitor/guest worthy of our attention, but that we have something to offer, too.

Hospitality begins with seeing and noticing the person in need of welcome. Shame always wants us to believe that we're invisible, unseen by others, that we have no voice, and that we do not deserve to be noticed. It is the most shame-filled men and women who find it hardest to meet the gaze of a friend or a counselor or a spouse. One friend's shame tells her that others only want to use her, and so she turns away. She is terrified to risk being known, so it feels safer to curl up into the corner of the chair and look down as she pours out details of repeated childhood sexual abuse. Another friend's shame of his past tells him he is not worthy of relationship to his wife, so he dares not lift his eyes to confirm the rejection he most fears. When these friends dare to look up, to look at you, will you be turned away in distraction? Or will you notice them and offer them welcome that starts with greeting them by name?

When you feel like them, will you courageously lift your head and act contrary to shame's lies?

God welcomes you by name. And he invites you into a community that will do the same. Shame begins to disappear when we are known, when our human dignity is honored, when we belong to a community of those practicing their redemption.

What to Do with Fear

Let's say that you begin to move out in risk-taking love in your community. You start to practice "one anothering" with those in your church, family, workplace, and neighborhood. You notice the presence of acceptance instead of judging, of truth-speaking rather than deception, of kind words replacing criticism and gossip. In return, others seem to be treating you better, too, and you feel encouraged to continue.

But then it happens. Someone, likely from your family or church, does not reciprocate. You have been moving along quite nicely with your shame-eradicating kindness campaign, and then it is thrown back in your face. Maybe it comes through unexpected criticism at work or home. Or you find yourself facing the type of person who triggers past experiences of shame. Maybe the coolest mom on the block joins your church, and she seems uncannily similar to the cheerleader who snubbed you in high school. Perhaps your new employer's demanding style takes you back to coaches or parents for whom your best was never enough.

Fear sets in, and you relationally freeze up, locked in shame. What now?

You need to be rescued. How about a "perfect love that drives out fear" (1 John 4:18)? Christ arrived on the scene of humanity to cast out your fear with the only perfect love available: the love of a perfect God. And it's even better: it's the love of a perfect God who initiates toward you first (1 John 4:19). He makes the first move—what security this brings! Our lagging, halfhearted responses, missteps, and sins are no match for a love of this magnitude. He loved you before you could acknowledge him; he wrote out every day of your life before you were born (Ps. 139:16); he did the unimaginable—dying a publicly shameful, excruciating death so that you might have life and love abundant.

In Christ-formed community, we are called to practice shame-eradicating love, but we will inevitably experience shame-confirming failure to love both from others and toward others. The fear we experience ultimately comes from fear of punishment or exclusion, or that our deepest insecurity might be validated—that I am not worthy of another's love and acceptance. This is why you are afraid to keep loving your wife; you know all too well the way her criticism wounds your heart. This is why you hold back from reaching out at church to ask for help. The last time you did that, you were given a pat answer and no follow through.

Into this fear of rejection and exclusion (the punishment of being relationally cut off from one another and God) comes the welcomed words of 1 John 4:18–19: "There is no fear in love, but perfect love casts out fear. For fear has to do with punishment, and whoever fears has not been perfected in love. We love because he first loved us." What casts out fear of love is a greater love that preexisted before our shame. A greater, weightier preexisting condition of God's love for his people— for you—came before any of your shame, and will follow you all the way into glory. We can love without fear for we are loved first. And so you can love first without expecting or requiring that love be returned. You are secure in the love of God for you in Christ. You are free to move out to experience fear-defying love through Christ as you practice perfect love that casts out fear. You will know freedom from the shame you dread as you love the one whose criticism or disappointment you fear. For even if the boss continues to ridicule, and the wife keeps on criticizing, and the church member cannot speak comfort to your suffering, you are free to keep loving, for *your love is not dependent on their response.*[6] You are joined to the community of the redeemed, held secure by a love that cannot be separated from us. God nailed his Son to a rugged, bloody piece of wood to ensure it.

"For I am sure that neither death nor life, nor angels nor rulers, nor things present nor things to come, nor powers, nor height nor depth, nor anything else in all creation, will be able to separate us from the love of God in Christ Jesus our Lord" (Rom. 8:38–39).

For Reflection and Discussion

1. When have you attempted to get rid of shame, or "vacuum it up"?

2. What aspects of shame-resisting community described by the Bible appeal to you the most?

3. How do you know someone is safe to turn to when you are struggling with shame or fear? Are you this kind of person? If not, what needs to change?

4. When has someone met you in the midst of your shame with words or actions of grace?

5. How does God's love drive out fear? How would believing this help you to love others even when they have disappointed you or when you are afraid?

3

Clothed in Christ: Body Shame

My weight/loss/gain since I was a child has tormented me. No amount of help has ever healed my pain about it.

Lady Gaga

In the spirit of bringing shame to light through community, I asked a small group of women to recall when they first felt ashamed of their bodies. Each woman recounted a memory, message, or defining event that contributed to a sense of body shame that she struggles with to this day. Patty described being an early bloomer, a feeling of shame at her developing breasts that makes her despise them even decades later. Lily said that even after losing significant weight, she still views herself as several sizes larger than she is and doesn't connect someone discussing "a thin woman" as describing her. Lauren remembered an almost casual gesture, her mom pointing out a slight facial imperfection and then seeking to brush it away. For years she wrestled with feeling imperfect—and that imperfect is not OK. All talked about the way the message seeps into our culture that anything less than a perfect body is a body to be ashamed of.

It's not only women who are haunted by body shame. Men, too, are increasingly pressured to achieve body perfection through well-developed physiques, and many men feel shame when they don't have the ideal body.[1] Today's media cruelly display weight gain or muscle loss. They laud extreme weight loss. And too often our cultures and communities and families and churches simply mirror what the media proclaim.

Body shaming can happen in obvious ways, like direct criticisms to a child about his or her weight or appearance. But it can also occur through our commentary on those around us. A daughter who hears her mom constantly scrutinize others' weight and appearance absorbs the message that acceptance and love and approval are tied to her weight. Imagine her struggle if she gains "the freshman fifteen" in college, or does not lose her baby weight postpartum. Even if her mom never says a word to her directly, the damage is done, and she may feel increased shame with her added pounds. A son who sees his father obsessively work out and praise those who are muscular and thin will likewise learn to tie approval to his image. Most of us are guilty of perpetuating a culture that puts physical beauty on a pedestal. Despite professing that "it's what inside that counts," how often do our children, nieces, nephews, and students hear us praise others for their character?

Maybe you don't struggle with your weight or body shape, but what about that least favorite physical characteristic of yours? You know, the one that you would pay good money to change if you could. Or perhaps you feel like you never know how to wear your hair, or do your makeup, or select clothes. All of these can attach to a broader definition of "body shame."

Body shame can take on generational overtones as well. The daughter who notices that her mom exercises for hours daily, always skimps on eating, and never eats dessert will buy into the message that this is how she, too, should treat her body. Research says that girls as young as first grade begin to desire to be thinner, and that by age ten, 84 percent of all children are afraid of being fat.[2] This is epidemic!

We grow up steeped in the cultural law that "thin/beautiful = good and loveable, and fat/unattractive = bad and rejected." Body shame is the feeling that your body with its imperfections is something of which to be ashamed—something you wish you could hide or change. But the reality is that we can never get away from our bodies, and there's really very little that can be changed about the bodies we are given. It's how we live in this world, clothed in our bodies. And so it is imperative that we address what to do with body shame, and how Jesus wants to clothe our body shame with his honor. Remember our working definition of shame: It's *the feeling of "not good enough," according to our own standard or our perception of* someone else's standard for us. It's what keeps us from being honest about our struggles, sins, and less-than-perfect moments. Fear of shame drives us to perfectionism in all areas of our lives, so that there would be no imperfection for others to notice and judge.

How We Try to Cover Our Body Shame

The ways that we seek to drive out body shame are many, and some are physically dangerous. [See appendix A for a detailed description and self-assessment of eating disorders.] The most common ways we seek to combat body shame include:

- Obsessive exercise and/or weight lifting
- Tightly managed rules for eating
- Expensive beauty products to combat wrinkles, aging, under-eye circles, etc.
- Fashionable clothing, which often comes at a high price
- Avoiding places where we will be physically exposed, like the pool or the beach

Each of these may help us to feel better about our bodies, at least temporarily. I feel exponentially better about myself when I'm wearing makeup and nice clothes. After indulging during holidays or a vacation, returning to the gym can help to shed those extra pounds I gained, or it at least helps me justify my excessive eating. Fashion and beauty products carry a high price tag because of an equally high demand for them—fed by us and our spending habits.

None of these are inherently unhealthy practices in moderation. Healthy eating and regular exercise are part of the way we practice good stewardship and care of the bodies we've been given. (And while I'm on the topic: I don't think decent quality clothing and beauty products are inherently bad.)

Yet there is a dark side to finding refuge from body shame in any of these practices alone. Eating disorders can form when healthy eating goes off track and when exercise becomes obsessive. Budgets and financial stewardship demand that we curb our spending on beauty products and clothing. Avoiding places of physical discomfort or exposure can become quite isolating when taken to an extreme. All of these practices offer at best a limited and fleeting solution to body shame.

They cannot fully heal body shame because it is not primarily a cultural problem or a self-image issue, but a heart condition for which we need massive inner transformation.

The "If Only" Game

Perhaps your struggle is more nuanced. You are not over-focused on your clothing, image, eating, or exercise habits, but you frequently play the "if only" game mentally: "If only _____, then I would be [happier/content/holier/more loving]." A few common ways this shows up for women in particular as it relates to issues of eating, appearance, and body weight are:

- "If only I knew what clothes were fashionable and had the budget to purchase them, then I would be more self-confident at parties and at church on Sunday mornings."
- "If only my hair were straighter/curlier/thinner/thicker, then I would be accepted by the 'in crowd.'"

- "If only I had fewer wrinkles and a flatter belly, then I would get asked out on dates or be pursued by my husband/or he would stop looking at pornography."
- "If only I were twenty pounds thinner, then I would be perpetually happy."

In all of these scenarios, we are saying that our physical appearance is the cause of current unhappiness, and that if we improve our physical appearance, life will change for the better. That's giving a lot of power to our bodies! No wonder we live pressured and pressuring others. No wonder the advertising agencies have a heyday playing into our self-doubt and misguided hope for a solution as they lure us with their promises of improved physical appearance. No wonder we are in debt chasing the lifestyle that we think will make us happier, while data reveals just the opposite.[3]

But before you throw out all your name-brand clothing, cancel your upcoming facelift, and swear off expensive clothing for the next decade, let's look a little deeper. Consider my twin daughters at age four, who loved nothing better than to twirl around and dance completely unself-consciously. They proudly showed me the fashionable outfits they had chosen: green polka-dotted socks peeking out of bright pink boots coordinated with red-and-purple striped sweaters and turquoise leggings. They beamed with the pleasure of self-confidence at my approval.

Somewhere along the way (as much as I will strive to fight its inevitability), my daughters will likely trade their exuberant self-confidence for insecure self-consciousness. Perhaps just a handful of adolescents make it through those tumultuous years without major hits to their previously positive view of themselves. What happens? Why the shift from happily twirling girls to painfully awkward teenagers?

In a word, *shame.*

Shame Begins in Childhood

As children grow into adolescents, the messages of shame that they receive from our culture and our families begin to soak in. Their social status depends on their style of clothes and hair, and they must be a particular size and shape in order to be loved and accepted. It's easy to point the finger at the media, but that won't tell the whole story. The most resilient men and women are still subject to the same media storm as everyone else. But many of them were given a shield to mitigate the shame thrown their way: a positive sense of self, nurtured by significant people in their lives. Most likely, their parents (or perhaps a doting aunt, caring grandparent, or parent-like substitute) have guided them to counteract the shame messages related to appearance.

I think about the way that my parents, and my dad in particular, never stopped adoring me even through the awkwardness of which our family photos are living proof. I was and am his "sunshine," and he freely gave me compliments about how pretty I was, and how he liked what I was wearing, and *wasn't I so beautiful, just like my mom?* In the midst of the firestorm that middle and high school were for me, I had a compass pointing to true north in the unconditional affirmation of my father. I never doubted whether he thought I was beautiful, and I never doubt it now. This was a secret weapon for a gangly, awkward girl finding her way in life through the unkind halls of high schools and cafeterias.

Fathers hold tremendous power in shaping their daughter's self-image, either to reinforce a sense of unworthiness or to provide a way to fight what she will encounter throughout her life. The father-daughter relationship communicates volumes about how she will be viewed by and interact with men. Is she valuable only because of her success and achievement and perfect physical appearance? Is she worth a man's attention and delight? When a father has been cold and distant, it is likely that a woman will struggle to understand God the Father as loving and welcoming. If a father is abusive, a daughter will carry deep wounds throughout her life. But if a father is generous with his affirmation and affection, he gives his daughter quite a gift: he points the way to the true Father, "from whom every family in heaven and on earth is named" (Eph. 3:15).

I am fully aware that many women struggle because they have parents who contribute to their body shame, as well as roommates, neighbors, childhood playmates, coaches, brothers, sisters, best friends, and husbands who have only amplified the message that feels hauntingly familiar. And right now, you may feel further from hope than when you started this chapter.

But regardless of how you have been (and are) buffeted and wounded by the waves of criticism and the subtle never-good-enough message that advertising is built upon, or how others (even parents) have added to your body shame, you have access to an *even better* secret weapon against the body shame you carry around daily.

Inside-Out Honor and Beauty

Take heart. The story gets better, and you're included in it. King David declares how God our Creator views and has created our bodies.

> For you formed my inward parts;
>> you knitted me together in my mother's womb.
> I praise you, for I am fearfully and wonderfully made.
> Wonderful are your works;
>> my soul knows it very well.
> My frame was not hidden from you,
> when I was being made in secret,
>> intricately woven in the depths of the earth.
> Your eyes saw my unformed substance;
> in your book were written, every one of them,
>> the days that were formed for me,
>> when as yet there was none of them. (Ps. 139:13–16)

David is speaking of an intimate knowledge of you, and a purposeful and physical knitting together of you from the time you were in your mother's womb to this present day. Your body is *wonderful* and *intricately woven*. As beautiful as the most radiant flower that you've ever seen—your beauty beats this a hundred times over. As strong as the strongest oak you've climbed or sat under—your strength is much more fearsome. How can this be true in a world of physical imperfections that we face daily in the mirror?

Could it be that we don't view ourselves accurately? We can't see from God's perspective. David knew that God sees from the inside out. When the priest Samuel went to anoint the next Israelite king, he assumed it would be one of David's older and more handsome brothers. God stopped Samuel in his tracks and said, "For the LORD sees not as man sees; man looks at the outward appearance, but the LORD looks at the heart" (1 Sam. 16:7). Then God introduces David, the poet who pens Psalm 139 about God's wonderful works in creating him. David elsewhere is called "a man after God's heart," and so what God saw within David was most important. Yet David was also able to praise God for his physical body, a body that we can assume was less handsome and strong than that of his other brothers.

Intricate means complex, complicated, and hard to understand.[4] This can apply to our bodies in so many ways. So-called "birth defects" and physical imperfections are included in this definition. Our bodies, even when limited by ill health or physical impairment, are infinitely complex. When trapped in body shame, we focus on what our bodies can't deliver for us instead of what our bodies can do and are doing for us. We limit their purpose to their appearance, and demand more when they bring us shame instead of the positive attention and admiration we crave. We forget the intricacy of our physical design. The way that our heart keeps pumping blood to each of our organs; the way we breathe without even thinking about it; how our digestive system processes food; all that it takes to move and stretch and walk and run. As you are reading this book right now, your brain is functioning on levels I cannot begin to describe, much less to comprehend.

Our bodies are fearfully and wonderfully made, not because they're perfectly beautiful on the outside, but because of how God designed for them to function and how they are meant to lead us to worship our Creator. He has given our bodies an inherent and inscribed value, which is vastly different from that of our culture and often our own hearts. Instead of our bodies leading us into worship of our Creator, our bodies become hindrances to God-worship and a source of other-worship or self-worship.

True Beauty Comes from Within

God speaks most directly about beauty when addressing the early church in a letter written by one of the first disciples of Jesus, Peter. Peter describes beauty in this way: "Let your adorning be the hidden person of the heart with the imperishable beauty of a gentle and quiet spirit, which in God's sight is very precious" (1 Pet. 3:4). How intriguing to think of "adorning" (dressing) yourself as something that comes from within—"the hidden person of the heart"! It's a beauty that never fades—imperishable—and it's precious in God's sight. It's a beauty described as gentle (or kind) and quiet (or peaceful). When we are chasing after beauty in clothing, cosmetics, thinness, wrinkle-free smiles, and shapely muscles, we are missing the ultimate beauty that God sees: that of our hearts.

We chase after the wrong beauty, and it eventually fails. It cannot clothe our shame, for it was never meant to do so. We need to be clothed by the imperishable beauty of Christ. He is our ultimate secret weapon. It's a beauty none of us can attain, but which we are given through faith in Jesus Christ. He was marred and physically disfigured, bearing our body shame to its full extent on the cross, so that we could be beautiful from the inside out. His is the gentle and quiet spirit that becomes ours through faith. It is the presence of the Holy Spirit within that we are to adorn ourselves with.

And so what are we to do with our longing for physical perfection? We must realize that it will come one day—but not through our futile striving. It will come when we are raised with Christ into the perfection of our resurrection bodies. All body shame will be eradicated as our bodies are raised in honor: "[The body] is sown in dishonor; it is raised in glory" (1 Cor. 15:43). This honor is retroactive, as we live in the days between Christ's past resurrection and our future resurrection with him. We can expect both the physical imperfection, dishonor, and shame that we'll carry until we die; and we can also expect the dispelling and redemption of body shame as we look forward in hope to the future honoring of our physical bodies. We will not return to the Edenic memory of "naked and unashamed" until we are resurrected anew in the new heavens and the new earth, clothed in our perfectly glorious bodies. And yet there are glimpses of physical glory even here—in the way we are all born into the world shameless and through redeemed sexuality in marriage. We see a small reflection of the physical reality of our unashamed destiny when watching a perfectly orchestrated ballet, or when a baby touches sand and sea for the first time, or when Olympic athletes compete in an event.

The next time you see a child dancing without shame, remember that this is where you began and where you are headed, through the hope of Jesus who was physically resurrected and in whose beauty we are even now clothed.

Getting Practical

You may be asking at this point, *But what does this really look like in my life?* For *me*, with my shame-laden stories of physical and verbal abuse, which I hold catalogued in my mind and stamped as body memories I can't seem to physically shake? For *me*, who never feels like I'm quite thin enough no matter how much I work out or how much weight I lose? For *me*, who cannot stand a certain part of my body—nose, arms, thighs, skin, hair? For *me*, who is battling disordered eating? For *me*, who overspends on clothes, cosmetics, and hair products? For *me*, whose confidence waxes and wanes depending on how good I feel like I look on any given day, for any given event?

What it really looks like is listening intently to God's words of love for you, and praying that you will begin to believe them. It includes sharing your story of body shame and your struggle against its lies with a trusted, safe friend, counselor, or pastor. It means asking for this safe person to speak truth to you. Remember: safe people are those who have shown you over time that they are trustworthy. They will affirm you, not criticize you. And they won't shy away from speaking the truth in gentle love to you either.

Not only do I need truthful reminders from friends about my situation (clothing, body image, beauty), but I need a call to confession from my God—a turning in repentance back toward him, an acknowledgment that yes, I have been chasing beauty in all the wrong places.[5] And where has that gotten me? Emptier than ever, more insecure, jealously comparing and competing, and far from my Father.

But he doesn't leave me there, and he hasn't left you there either. The Father comes to heal your body shame by giving you a new heart (Ezek. 26:36). This may be the last thing you think you need, but it's actually the first and most important thing. The new heart you're given through faith in Jesus Christ is a heart that can't be swayed by fashion trends and vacillating weight or body shape. This new heart gives you an unshakeable beauty, one that can never perish, spoil, or fade— an "imperishable beauty." This heart knows love and speaks love to you constantly, comforting pained places inside of you. Christ died and rose again so that you would always know that you're loved, and so that nothing could separate you from his love (Rom. 8:38–39). Not even your body shape or disordered eating or appearance obsession can keep you from God's love. None of it holds a candle to the love you have through Christ with the Father.

So try it—hold up your false refuges to the light of this love and see how they compare. Which of these has sacrificed for you, or is it that they ask you to sacrifice for them? All of them promise love—but have any of them delivered on that promise? Isn't it more likely that they made love feel more elusive than before?[6] For even if you obtained the love you sought through their means—becoming your ideal weight, learning how to dress and wear your makeup and do your hair—doesn't that leave you more insecure than before? And wouldn't this heap pressure on you to keep up appearances to maintain the love you seek?

When you see the false refuges for what they are and what your heart goes after instead of Jesus, only one refuge from your body shame remains: arms stretched wide on the cross, inviting you into divine love at the cost of Christ's broken and torn body. What God gives you is love with truth—a truth that is not adulterated by today's "thin equals beautiful" culture. He restores the true definition of beauty as we are restored in his image. Just as Eve considered eating the forbidden fruit that was pleasing to the eye, we too buy into assigning value based on outer appearances, exchanging "beauty" for just "pretty." But Jesus sees true beauty differently than fallen humanity sees it. Would you believe he sees you as more beautiful than the magazine photo? The magazine photo has been airbrushed and retouched—it is no longer "truth," but made pleasing to the eye. You are who you are, flaws and all, and you need a Redeemer. Marred by the fall as we may be, we are still created in God's image and reflect his intrinsic value. What does he give you instead of your shame? Clothing and identity and unshakeable eternal confidence. This begins to change *everything*, and soon you're walking with your head held high because you know you are loved and that you are beautiful.

For Reflection and Discussion

1. What messages have shaped the way you view your body? Who or what has most contributed to your body shame?

2. How do you think you have impacted your friends, children, spouse, or coworkers through your mind-set and/or comments you've made about physical beauty and appearance?

3. Which "if only" statement(s) connects most with you? Is there another one you would add to the list?

4. What is God's definition of beauty according to 1 Peter 3:4 and Psalm 139? How do we increase this type of beauty?

5. What could it look like for you to live free of body shame? What would you do differently for an hour (or a day or a week)?

4

United to Christ: Social Shame

Fitting in is about assessing a situation and becoming who you need to be to be accepted. Belonging, on the other hand, doesn't require us to *change* who we are; it requires us to *be* who we are.

Brené Brown

I've often felt like an outsider. Three's not company, and my two younger brothers often left me out of activities like mountain biking and G.I. Joe playing. I attempted to join in at times, but I have about zero athleticism and preferred Barbies to action figures. Being a Christian teenager in a public high school that had very few other Christians added to my sense of exclusion. Then this Southern girl attended a Midwestern college, and although I felt accepted, I still felt a little bit on the outside of the Midwest culture. This paled in comparison to my experience living in Philadelphia during seminary. Talk about a cross-cultural experience for someone raised in South Carolina! Being a woman at seminary also put me in the minority, despite finding great camaraderie with fellow female counseling students. We bonded together because of our common sense of exclusion.

The label of "outsider" is one manifestation of what I call *social shame*. Social shame is when you feel ridiculed or excluded by a group or person to which you want to belong. Its opposite is being fully known and accepted as you are, for who you are.

Like me, you can probably recall at least one to two experiences of feeling rejected or on the "outside" when you craved nothing more than acceptance and welcome—a sense of belonging. Where is it that you experience it right now? Let's also consider the way that social media has amplified both our desire to belong, and our fear/experience of rejection.

Social Media: The Trap of Comparison

Imagine this scenario: You have had an amazing day with your family on vacation at the beach cottage you rent every year, and before you turn off the light, you decide to pop in to Instagram or Facebook just to check in, and perhaps also to share one of the beautiful beach pictures from your day. What you see on social media turns you jealous and envious in an instant. Your neighbors' picture from their tropical Caribbean vacation causes you to look around and notice how shabby the beach cottage now seems. Your sister's picture of her happy family makes you hyperaware of the simmering conflict with your daughter for which you want resolution. Or, worst of all, you see a picture of many of your close friends gathered at an event to which you weren't even invited. Never mind that you wouldn't have been able to go—but not to hear about it at all? And for them to plan it while you're away? You feel crushed.

What changed your contented enjoyment of your beach vacation? Part of it is that most of us use social media to show only the best parts of our lives, and so what we see of each other is distorted. As a result, when you see another's images, you feel like your life pales in comparison and discontentment raises its ugly head. It's a phenomena supported by a host of researchers—they've observed a correlation between social media usage and loneliness. Loneliness increases the more a person uses social media.[1]

But the problem isn't with social media. It's with how social media activates our social insecurities and our heart's default to compare and compete because we feel like we deserve better than what we're getting. We are not content with who we are and what we have been given. Social media provides an accelerated means of revealing our hearts. But it's not the fault of social media. The fault lies with how we use it and respond to what we see on it. We often use social media as a shield against our shame, but we always come up short because it isn't powerful enough to rescue us. And what we see via social media can trigger our shame in potent ways, resurrecting long-held insecurities and fears of exclusion.

A Definition of Social Shame

See if you recognize these hallmarks of social shame in yourself:

- *Insecurity.* The inner belief that you will never belong to anyone or be at home in any place, which shows up in constant self-doubt and hesitancy when making decisions.
- *People-pleasing.* Insecurity feeds into people-pleasing, and people-pleasing feeds into insecurity. The more you try to gain acceptance with the people around you, the more insecure you will feel because it requires a constant chameleon-like flexibility on your part.
- *Fear of intimacy.* The more you try to be what you think other people want you to be, the less you will be able to be who you are. And so you will be afraid of allowing anyone to get close enough to expose that you don't know who you are. You will find ways to keep people at arm's length so that they are impressed by you without knowing you. Or you may close people out entirely through a stoic, hard shell. Or you may be so good at connecting with other people and caring for *them*, that no one thinks to ask *you* how you're doing or to care for you. Author Emily Freeman describes it this way: "In my silence and refusal to be vulnerable, I inadvertently taught [others] that I had no needs, no weakness, and no reason to lean on [them]. . . . You have trained people to think you have no needs, but you are secretly angry with them for believing you."[2]
- *Fear of rejection.* Insecurity leads to people-pleasing, which is often motivated by fear of intimacy, which is motivated by fear of rejection. If no one truly knows you, no one can

reject you. If you don't (or can't) allow others to get close to you, they cannot come to a place of choosing *not* to know you. You can't be asked to leave a place you have never yourself entered.

C. S. Lewis captured our dilemma well in *The Four Loves*:

> To love at all is to be vulnerable. Love anything and your heart will be wrung and possibly broken. If you want to make sure of keeping it intact, you must give your heart to no one, not even to an animal. Wrap it carefully round with hobbies and little luxuries; avoid all entanglements; lock it up safe in the casket or coffin of your selfishness. But in that casket—safe, dark, motionless, airless—it will change. It will not be broken; it will become unbreakable, impenetrable, irredeemable.[3]

Disentangling from the Web of Social Shame

How on earth will you get disentangled from such a web? How do you deal with the shame triggers that keep you securely locked in your tower of one? Ann reaches out to invite a new friend over for coffee, and when she says no, Ann feels crushed and rejected. John takes the risk to initiate conversation with an attractive coworker, and when she snubs him, he feels like he's back in middle school alone on the dance floor watching everyone else flit by happily. Sandra shares in her small group at church how alone she's felt since her husband left her, and no one follows up the next week. In their attempts to break free of the shame that isolates them, they all end up feeling more alone than before, and more shame-filled than ever. "Excluded and rejected: OUTSIDER," seems like a social brand they'll never escape.

Every relationship is a risk at some level. The risk that you will be known for who you are opens you up to the risk that you will then be rejected and placed outside of the circle of secure relationship for which you crave. It feels much safer to put your efforts and energies into trying to be who others would like you to be, and there is no shortage of opinions *there*. It feels more secure, ironically enough, to remain in a place of insecurity, catering to the whims of those around you and fueling the fears of intimacy and rejection by keeping them at bay (so you think). Brené Brown says it well in distinguishing between fitting in and belonging: "Fitting in is about assessing a situation and becoming what you need to be to be accepted. Belonging, on the other hand, doesn't require us to *change* who we are; it requires us to *be* who we are."[4]

Because I resonated with the constant quest to fit in, I was drawn to the 1990's romantic comedy, *Runaway Bride*, starring Julia Roberts. The bride put on varying personas to match her suitors, but all of her engagements ended with her fleeing the groom before or at the altar. In every case, she experienced a moment of haunting truth—that *this* wasn't who she really was—and so she ran away—and found another relationship. The cycle continued until she was finally brave enough to be alone for a while. A poignant scene toward the end of the movie shows her tasting eggs that have been prepared in a variety of ways so that she could discover which style *she* preferred; she had so adapted her preferences to the man-of-the-month that she couldn't even identify her own culinary tastes.

At this point, a practical exercise might be to put this book down and delve into a self-study of your likes and dislikes and find out who you are. For some, this may be part of God's path away from insecurity, people-pleasing, and fear of intimacy and rejection. It was part of my own journey the first time I sought counseling. My counselor encouraged me that it was OK to find out who I was, and that as a Christian, knowing myself better could even help me to know God better. She quoted John Calvin, who wrote: "True and sound wisdom, consists of two parts: the knowledge of God and of ourselves."[5]

Yet I need to give a disclaimer at this point, because part of our problem as Westerners is that we have exclusively defined ourselves as individuals *apart from* community. Elizabeth Gilbert of *Eat, Pray, Love* fame claims that she did not find herself until she left her husband and her marriage behind.[6] This is *not* the type of self-discovery that I am suggesting. Instead, I invite you into a place where you are alone with your heavenly Father as a daughter or a son. Lay your heart bare before him, letting the deepest cries of your heart be heard. Let's pay attention to our desires not for the purpose of being led *away* from God, but in order to be led *closer* to God and to others.

Risking Your Way Out of Isolation to Community

Why would I ask you to do such a risky thing as to voice your desires and to confess your insecurities before God? Because I am confident that God is the first and only safe confidant.

Social shame asks the questions: *Where do I belong? Who am I? Who are my people? Who can be trusted?* None of these questions can or will be answered perfectly by any person, place, community, or church. Your experience tells you this truth.

But the truth is that in order to be in safe, secure relationships within safe and secure communities and churches, someone has to go first. Someone has to take the risk, the plunge, into vulnerability. It's the only hope of connection. I cannot empathize with pain that I do not know about—that you have hidden from me or others. One troubling aspect of the modern-day church in America is that there are few people who are brave and courageous enough to risk going first (which contributes to the church's reputation as a community where it's not safe to be real and vulnerable). The trailblazer always has a more difficult time than those who follow.

The problem then is how will you have courage to be the trailblazer, to pioneer your way forward past the relational barriers shame creates between us, barriers of fear and insecurity and people-pleasing? There is only one I know who can make us brave enough for such a task—who can give us the honor and secure belonging we desire. He is the one who made the way for us to return to God—who repaired the sin-broken trail of relationship to God through his life, death, and resurrection on our behalf. Jesus said, "I am the way, and the truth, and the life" (John 14:6), and then did the impossible so that we could live courageously in relationship with God and lead the way in restoring relationships with others. Jesus was excluded by all and abandoned by his friends in a time of need so that we could always be welcomed into relationship. At his greatest hour of pain and separation, even God himself turned his back on him. God's "Beloved Son, in whom I am well pleased" became the one who alone cried out, "My God, my God! Why have you forsaken me?" (Matt. 3:17; 17:5; 27:46). God rejected Jesus in a moment of agony on the cross in order that we would be eternally embraced through faith in this sacrificed Savior.

Jesus's closest friends on earth, his disciples, abandoned him when they fell asleep during his hour of greatest need, and then fearfully fled as soon as he was arrested. Trailblazing the way to salvation was a lonely path, filled with social shame as Jesus was repeatedly rejected and abandoned.

What motivated him? It was love and joy. Hebrews talks about "the joy that was set before him," which helped him to "endure the cross, despising the shame," and which led him to the victorious, secure place where he "is seated at the right hand of the throne of God" (Heb. 12:2). This throne is described no longer as a throne of judgment, but a throne of grace—where we may receive help in our time of need (Heb. 4:16). And, oh, how we need help! How needy we are! We need grace to first admit how much we need it. Ephesians 2:8 says that even this is a gift of God—faith to believe in grace. And we need courage to believe we have the grace for which we ask.

When you cry out to this Savior—this made-vulnerable-to-you one—he is quick to answer. There is no waiting for a response, as we must do with every other person. Even the most attentive friend, spouse, roommate, or parent is not available 24/7. God gives us the Holy Spirit through Jesus who is interceding for us even when we sleep (Rom. 8:26–27; Heb. 7:25). Jesus is ready and waiting for you to call on him. This perfect love begins to drive out your fear of shame. That's what social shame is at its core. It is fear of being shamed, of experiencing relational rejection or exclusion. Andy Crouch writes, "Shame is always seen and recognized by the community. Social shame, as well as honor, is all too obvious to all concerned."[7] Add to this Ed Welch's words in *Shame Interrupted*: "At the very heart of shame is the absence of relationships, the absence of being known, personal isolation."[8] God never excludes you, but is always calling out for you and seeking to know you; and he has made you part of a community where you have eternal belonging.

From Insecurity to True Confidence: A Place to Belong

Though I appeared confident and carefree in my college years, inside I was as insecure as I was in fourth grade. I had simply learned how to mask it better. I remember feeling afraid of who to talk to when walking into a crowded party, and I remember the butterflies in my stomach when I knew that a guy I wanted to impress would be present. I paid close attention to what I wore, how I laughed, and what I said. I felt the most confident if I could enter surrounded by good friends. They were like my emotional bodyguards. With them beside me, I could face anything or anyone. I could appear confident and free of fear.

The occasions when I had to attend a social event alone were quite different. I remember bolstering myself with this verse: "I have set the LORD always before me; because he is at my right hand, I shall not be shaken" (Ps. 16:8).

Doesn't this speak right into the midst of our insecurity, people-pleasing, fear of intimacy, and fear of rejection?

1. *I have set the Lord always before me.* I am therefore secure. He has blazed the trail for me, and I connect with his work and security through faith.
2. Not only is he before me, but *he is at my right hand.* I am therefore in the most intimate of relationships without possibility of rejection. He becomes my constant "emotional bodyguard."
3. And so I can conclude with the psalmist, *I shall not be shaken* by fears within or without, nor by who I think others wish I could be.

Living out this truth takes faith and courage to resist shame whenever it whispers its lies of rejection to your heart. At least you know where the map begins, or rather, whom to follow down the path that the map lays out for you.

A Few Practical Suggestions: From Excluded to Welcoming

Once you address the fear of exclusion and exposure, the heart of your social shame, you are free to engage differently in groups, gatherings, and social media. Your focus can become, "How can I include and welcome others as I myself have been included and welcomed?" And you can do this even in the middle of the very groups where you've felt excluded.

One word of caution: If your attempts at initiating relationship have been *repeatedly* ignored, it could be wise to find a different group in which you can practice shame-resilient relationships. Some families, churches, and small groups simply aren't ready to accept people who are transparent about their imperfections and real about their struggles. Pray for change, and seek advice as to whether you should be part of the change. But in the meantime, also pursue another group where you can connect with others who are willing to engage with you on the journey away from being controlled by social shame.

Social media is incredibly potent for social shame, both through providing new ways to be publicly shamed and in highlighting feelings of rejection and discontentment. If you wonder how much it has reinforced your experience of social shame, disconnect for a day or a week and watch how you respond. Many people report feelings of withdrawal not dissimilar from a drug detox as well as increased insecurity.[9] This might signal that social media has fed your fear of exclusion rather than being a healthy way to connect with others. What if instead you began to use social media as a way to enhance authentic relationships? What if you chose to share what's closer to real life than the airbrushed life stories our social media accounts usually portray? If you are really daring, ask a friend who knows you well in real life how similar your online presence is to who you are. And if you're feeling especially courageous, write a post about how you are *really* doing.

Here is a good exercise in walking free of social shame

to practice in your closest relationships: Be committed to authenticity, and become a safe person with whom others can be authentic.

- How do you respond when a friend or family member is transparent with you?
- Do you receive what is shared without offering immediate judgment or advice?
- Do you ask further questions to help you understand?
- Do you affirm their courage in being honest with you?
- If you feel at a complete loss in how to respond, can you communicate this and ask them how they'd like for you to respond?
- When you get it wrong, or they do, will you speak honestly and offer gracious space and a listening ear?

Imagine a community where we are free to be known and seen for who we are on our best days and our worst days. Imagine a place where others are always welcomed, regardless of how different they appear from the majority. We will not experience this perfectly until we reach our true home when Jesus returns to right every wrong, but we who know him belong in him now and are called to create communities where others can taste true welcome and shame-free belonging. Because we belong to the King of the universe, we belong wherever we go. There is an eternal home being prepared for us, to which we will one day arrive despite our doubts and fears of exclusion. This contradicts our social shame at the core of our identity, giving us courage to offer the belonging of which we ourselves are certain.

For Reflection and Discussion

1. When have you felt like an outsider? How did you respond? Did anything change in your status to make you feel included or welcomed?

2. How has social media served to activate or expose your insecurities?

3. Describe the four hallmarks of social shame. How do these play out in your life?

4. What has God done through Jesus Christ to give us a place to belong? How should this change our communities? How can you be part of what needs to be changed?

5

Free in Christ: Performance Shame

> Many people pursue success as a way to overcome the sense that they are somehow "outsiders." If they attain it, they believe, it will open the doors into the clubs, into the social sets, into relationships with the connected and influential. Finally, they think, they will be accepted by all the people that matter. Success promises to do that, but in the end it cannot deliver.
>
> Timothy Keller

A family member retells the story from decades past with crystal-clear clarity: "It was a beautiful fall day when I was finally sworn in as an attorney, having slogged my way through three years of law school and about six grueling weeks of intense study for the Bar exam, which lasted three days. We gathered on the sun-drenched steps in front of the State Supreme Court building with our parents and loved ones to bask in the glory of the achievement. That's when my dad looked at me with a smile on his face and said, 'Son, I never thought you would make it.' That stung because it came from a heart that really didn't believe in me. A few years later at a family wedding reception, I overheard my dad say to another guest, 'If my son had not found Christ, he probably would be in jail now.' That was probably true, but what a deflating comment to hear from my own father. Grace has richly given me the ability to forgive and overlook his back-handed compliments, but the heart has a deep memory for such things."

Despite the fact that this family member is now well-respected in his profession, and his father has long since passed away, his father's condemning and shaming words illustrate how futile even our best performances are to conquer or silence the shame from our worst critics.

I often feel plagued by personal demons of perfectionism in the pressure to produce. It can at times be crippling. But in God's mercy, he has given me the task of writing about what I myself am continually practicing. In the constellation that I will name "performance shame," you will find perfectionism, fear of failure, pressure to perform, self-righteousness, procrastination, criticism of self and others, and/or lack of creativity. They all fit together, and one easily leads and then develops into another.

Start with pressure to perform. Why do we feel the pressure to perform? We are *afraid of failure*, defined as not measuring up to our own personal standards and those of others. Why are we afraid of failure? We feel like we should be the best at everything we attempt, and that we are in fact better than others (*self-righteousness*). So then we *procrastinate* what we fear will be inevitable failure and self-disappointment And often underneath the procrastination is criticism, which stifles creativity. When we are anticipating what the critic will say about our work proposal, report, project, art, essay, or article, we tend to put off the inevitable failure that we fear is lurking at completion. To engage in our work and calling with all we are, and to continue without stalling out or freezing up requires silencing the critic within (because too often it is our own voice that speaks the loudest words of condemnation). One application of the Bible's command to "judge not, that you be not judged" seems to be the reality that the harsher I am toward others, the harsher I will be toward myself—as well as vice versa. This command is part of our rescue and our freedom: God rescues us from the critic within so that we would be free to creatively engage our corner of the world/work he's given to us.

Brené Brown summarizes her research on the connection between perfectionism and creativity this way: "Perfectionism crushes creativity—which is why one of the most effective ways to start recovering from perfectionism is to start creating."[1] She defines perfectionism as:

> The belief that if we do things perfectly and look perfect, we can minimize or avoid the pain of blame, judgment, and shame. Perfectionism is a twenty-ton shield that we lug around, thinking it will protect us, when in fact it's

the thing that's really preventing us from being seen. . . . Perfectionism is not self-improvement. Perfectionism is, at its core, about trying to earn approval. Most perfectionists grew up being praised for achievement and performance (grades, manners, rule following, people pleasing, appearance, sports). Somewhere along the way, they adopted this dangerous and debilitating belief system: "I am what I accomplish and how well I accomplish it. Please. Perform. Perfect." Healthy striving is self-focused: How can I improve? Perfectionism is other-focused: What will they think?[2]

Perfectionistic striving keeps us from working hard on a project in order to fully utilize our creative capacities, and instead drives us to obsess over a project as we think about how our boss and colleagues may criticize it. Perfectionism seeks to remove any possibility of criticism from every aspect of performance.

Mine is a story of striving and trying to be perfect as I receive just enough praise, approval, and recognition along the way to feed my addiction to people-pleasing as I pursue that ever-elusive mark of "perfect." As a counselor, I've learned that I am not the only one who struggles with perfectionism and worries or obsesses over performance. One client is an attentive mom who also works part time outside the home. She experiences sleepless nights and constant anxiety because she is worried that she is not doing enough. Her boss demands more and more, and so do her kids. She has structured a life that looks balanced, but she feels continually pulled by the inward strain of her own perfectionism. If her boss criticizes anything, she redoubles her efforts to produce perfection. If a child gets less than a glowing report card, she meets with the teacher to ask how she should be doing more at home. She rarely allows herself rest, because rest can come only once perfection has been achieved. But perfection is an ever-elusive goal, one that keeps moving the closer you seem to approach it.

Another friend feels shame in being unemployed. Who is he without his job? With an abundance of time to reflect on his life, he grows depressed. His days feel meaningless, and when his wife returns home from her job, he dreads the question of what he did all day. Sure, the house is clean, the laundry is folded, and dinner is cooked, but this does not seem like enough. He remembers his important job and obsessively sends out applications for positions that barely interest him. *Something* would be better than nothing.

A Definition of Performance Shame

Performance shame comes from trying to perform for the wrong audience—those around us. It comes from the lie that our work, success, and accomplishments are what we need to feel good about ourselves. Performance shame makes us think that our worth is tied to our performance, and when we are plagued by performance shame, *everything* becomes a performance. Underneath we are asking the questions, Am I loved? Have I done enough to belong? Do I have value apart from my contributions and work? We begin to play the *if only* game, with approval and self-confidence and relaxation coming after we achieve the next thing. The basic formula becomes:

(1) If only:

- I get a job promotion.
- My kids grow up happy and well-adjusted.
- I'm successful in ministry.
- My children succeed in sports and/or school.
- I academically achieve the next degree or accolade.
- I retire with enough funds to live comfortably.
- My parents tell me, "Well done!"
- My adult child recognizes all that I sacrificed in staying home.

(2) Then I will know that I am loved, valuable, and have a place to belong and can rest from striving to do and to offer more.

It may feel hopeless to recognize how much we need others' approval for every endeavor in our lives. Our culture attempts to speak to this by saying, "Find people who always approve of you. Focus on your areas of competence and avoid areas of failure." Yet it feels empty, doesn't it? Truth be told, few people in our lives will always approve of us. It's hard to find areas of competence, and all of us wrestle with failure—or the perception of failure—even in areas where we are competent. Some factors in life are beyond our control, like the impossible-to-please boss or the parent who's never satisfied even when we are doing our best. Our Western culture has not given us hope that we can change despite being wired with perfectionist tendencies and while surrounded by the criticism often found in the workplace, home, or church. Strategies to manage better, simplify more, and increase efficiency abound, but they tend to leave us *more* tired, worn out, and shame-laden instead of less so. God provided the freedom we need through a costly solution—a life lived perfectly in exchange for our imperfections, to give us the gift of undeserved rest.

How God Interrupts the Cycle of Performance Shame

God speaks directly into our performance shame with two truths:

1. We have been living for the wrong person.

2. We have been seeking approval through the wrong means.

D. A. Carson says that we do not lie awake at night recounting the ways we think we have brought shame to God through our actions; what keeps us anxious and sleepless are the ways that we feel shame before others. The *I can't believe I said that to her!* sort of thinking is what we mull over. Or the *Maybe I failed that exam, or received that academic rejection, but once I try this . . . then I will have arrived.* Carson exposes that we have missed the cause for deeper shame, a shame of being exposed before God and the shame of our attempts to cover up our shame. Perhaps we obsess over these smaller shame moments because we cannot face our real shame problem: that we live ashamed to walk and talk openly with our Creator.[3]

We are Adam and Eve, hiding when God pursues us and seeking to cover up with the closest thing near us, which in our Western culture is often our achievements and performance. We feel exposed before God, but it is easier to say,

"I feel naked [exposed] in front of him, and so I will hide from him and blame him for my shame." We play the ultimate shame- and blame-shifting game begun by Adam in the garden of Eden. "It was Eve—'she gave me the fruit of the tree, and I ate'" (Gen. 3:12). And then when God turns to Eve, she blames the Serpent who "deceived me, and I ate" (v. 13).

At this point, God does not blast Eve or Adam for their blame-shifting. First and foremost, he curses the Serpent, who is Satan in disguise. Eve told the truth about the Devil's deception, and God responds by cursing evil. But he does not stop there. God can see through their self-deception, and he confronts both Eve and Adam, calling them to account for their own choices to be deceived and led astray. As descendants of Adam and Eve, we experience grave consequences every day of our lives: futility in work, and frustration in marriage and child-bearing and relationship.

Not only does God confront Adam and Eve, but God provides for their real shame. He promises Jesus Christ. And when we look forward in redemptive history, we find the hope to cover our deepest shame of our insufficient performance being exposed before God. Isaiah rightly says that even our best attempts, our righteous acts, or even our ministry pursuits are like "a polluted garment" before God (Isa. 64:6) if they're done to try to earn God's approval and good standing before him. The things we do to try to cover up our shame bring us more shame than before. We feel like our work isn't up to par, so we spend increasing amounts of time at the office and less time at home. As a result, our family relationships disintegrate while work continues to move the bar higher and higher up and out of reach. We now add the shame of failing at family to the shame of work performance. Or we feel exposed that we have not been good enough to outweigh our sins before God. We increase our involvement at church or in our community, showing up at every service project, and begin to look down on all of those who seem less committed than we are. Now we have added self-righteousness to our sins, with the additional danger of feeling better about ourselves because of our religious performance while we are further away from true devotion to God. We desperately need to be rescued.

Rescue comes only through Jesus. Jesus took the shame of our shame-filled (and shame-fueled) performances and misplaced blame, and bore it in his body and shed blood for us on the cross. He covered not only the guilt of our sin, but also the shame of trying to cover up our sin. And the good news does not stop there! We have Jesus's righteous performance *in place of our feeble half-hearted attempts.* "For our sake he [God] made him [Jesus] to be sin who knew no sin, so that in him we might become the righteousness of God" (2 Cor. 5:21).

God looked into our people-pleasing, perfectionist hearts that crave ever-elusive approval, and he traded all of that for Jesus's blameless performance on our behalf. Everything true of Jesus is true of us. Colossians says that our life is *hidden with Christ in God* and that this is our hope of glory (Col. 3:4 and 1:27). *Glory* is shorthand for all the approval and honor and recognition we've been seeking all of our lives through our performance and achievements and relational finesse. Glory is ours not because of our accomplishments but because of Jesus. In union with Jesus through faith, we have the stamp of the Father's eternal love and approval. The only performance needed is Jesus's work of salvation on our behalf.

Healing Performance Shame

In light of these great truths—that we are perfect without trying to be, and perfectly loved despite our imperfect performance—how can we be healed of our performance shame? Here is a picture of what healing can look like:

1. *Coming to the end of your capacity.* Recognize your limits and the impossibility of living up to perfection.
2. *Embracing imperfection.* Stop trying to cover it up or to pretend it doesn't exist. Talk about it with safe friends; write about it; ask your small group to pray for your *real* struggles; post an image on social media of your messy kitchen or closet and tag it with #embracingimperfection.[4] In doing so, you're inviting others to join you in stepping off the performance treadmill.
3. *Letting criticism refine you instead of define you.* Criticism wakes us up to how much we have been living for the wrong audience. We will always run into critics in whatever we do, so let the criticism lead you back to your secure identity of *loved and perfect because of Jesus.*
4. *Changing your audience.* This naturally flows from criticism, but you don't have to wait for the critic to jolt you awake. Who are you working and living for? Anyone other than God will bring insecurity and shame in its wake. In contrast, God sings over you with delight (Zeph. 3:17),

beams with the pride of an approving parent, calls you "my beloved," and says your life work is part of the poem he's writing in the world (Eph. 2:10). "Being [God's] workmanship . . . means we are all poems, individual created works of a creative God. And this poetry comes out uniquely through us as we worship, love, pray, rest, work, and exist."[5]

5. *Risking authenticity through telling our stories.* Glennon Melton, author of *Carry On, Warrior*, and a popular mom-blogger, introduces herself to audiences by saying, "I'm Glennon, and I'm a recovering everything."[6] She has a tremendous following because her courage inspires others to the same. She is living authentically, risking rejection, and yet receiving true welcome as well. Expect both rejection and welcome when you begin to live and share authentically. Some may turn away, but others will draw closer.

6. *Resting before your work's done.* The Christian practice of Sabbath—six days of work to one day of rest—is particularly difficult for those of us who define ourselves by our work. But as one Sunday school teacher shared, "The only person whose work was finished on earth was Jesus." Our work won't ever be completed, and we cannot put off rest until our work is done.

Free to Rest

What if we lived like that today? For the next five minutes, or the next five days? How might this change our frenetic pace of life? Who are you when you've lost your job, retired, or failed in parenting or marriage? Your identity is not in what you do but in who you are. We are God's beloved through faith in

Jesus, and in us God is well-pleased. We cannot ultimately and eternally fail before God because Jesus did not fail. "It is finished" was his cry from the cross (John 19:30). We are forever righteous before a holy God. And so we are free from being defined by criticism, both our own or that from others. We can do the next brave or creative action we fear *now*, without putting it off another day or minute or hour. We are free to live out the creativity that resides deep in our souls, stifled perhaps by years of neglect and covered by layers of disdain. We are free to give priority to those whom we profess to be most important to us rather than run around harried and hurried by our work and service obligations. We can call it quits and turn in the "good-enough" project or assignment without perfecting it to death. We are free to parent according to who God has made us to be, not who we think we *should* be.

We are free to respond to Jesus's new and surprising work ethic that begins with rest. He invites us in Matthew 11:28, "Come to me, all who labor and are heavy laden, and I will give you rest." This rest is a freedom from our striving, which includes the rhythm of Sabbath as part of our "work week." We can rest while work remains incomplete and unfinished. We can plan a vacation without feeling guilty. We are to enjoy our time and days off because our soul and body need them.

So what are we waiting for? Permission? Approval? Recognition? We have it already in Christ, whose invitation to rest concludes with: "Take my yoke upon you, and learn from me, for I am gentle and lowly in heart, and you will find rest for your souls. For my yoke is easy, and my burden is light" (Matt.

11:29–30). If your burden feels heavy, consider that you might be carrying the wrong burden—one of performance shame and perfectionism—rather than the light burden of your imperfect performance being traded for Jesus's perfection and righteousness. Only with such a light load can we freely rest and rightly work, not to *be* loved, but because we *are* loved.

For Reflection and Discussion

1. Describe how perfectionism and performance shame connect. In what areas of your life do you seek to be perfect? What are you afraid of if you are not perfect (or come up short) in these areas?
2. What is your "if only" in terms of striving to do or achieve in order to be loved and accepted?
3. When did the message of performance being tied to love and acceptance first emerge in your life?
4. How does Jesus's performance free you to rest from your striving?

6

Response to Shame

Hope is a steely confidence that God is in this story
of shame and he is up to something good.

Ed Welch

Isn't it true that vision is what keeps us slogging through the
sometimes grueling process inherent to any transformation? I
think about the summer day in Ireland when the thought of
reaching the summit to soak in a panoramic view of green,
rolling hills overcame my innate aversion to hiking up a steep
mountain. Unfortunately on that particular afternoon, the
clouds and rain obscured the view and made a difficult hike
feel impossible. I don't remember anything beautiful about
the summit, but I do remember a fair amount of complain-
ing (on my part) and my friends seeking to encourage me to

keep going. I did—but it did not feel very rewarding. The only accomplishment I felt was relief that this experience was behind me.

The upward journey against shame can feel similar, and it often lasts a lifetime. Yet we are in good company. The words of Hebrews 12:1–2 are instructive: "Therefore, since we are surrounded by such a great cloud of witnesses, let us also lay aside every weight, and the sin which clings so closely, and let us run with endurance the race that is set before us, looking to Jesus, the founder and perfecter of our faith, who for the joy that was set before him endured the cross, despising the shame, and is seated at the right hand of the throne of God." Life is a race uniquely marked out for each of us, where we can expect weights and sin as well as joy. Our joy comes from looking to Jesus's joy that empowered his endurance *and* his despising of shame. Could it be that shame then is at cross-purposes with joyful endurance? Is shame part of the weight that we need to cast off in our race set before us? Responding to shame requires looking to Jesus, who despised shame, who covered our shame, who frees us to run with joyful endurance. Shame hinders us in the race. So how are we to throw off shame?

A Better Narrative Than My Shame-Laden Story

I am saturated in shame. Body shame shows up each time I try on a pair of pants that has become a bit too snug, or every time I see a picture of my slimmer self before my body bore the changes that twin pregnancy brought. Social shame rears its ugly head in the insecurities I often feel when in a new group, or when I go to the gym or to church or to a party. I feel excluded from my friends' enviable lives when I check Facebook or Instagram. Performance shame riddles me each time I see how many unanswered emails sit waiting for me in my inbox, or when I pass the dust-covered side table. It haunts me right after I submit an article or teach a lesson or write another chapter. I immediately begin thinking of all the ways I need to change what I wrote or said so that I won't be criticized.

Shame is everywhere. How can I escape it? Each emotion I feel gets connected or tainted with shame if I let it. I can feel ashamed when I am resentful toward my family, or shame for feeling happy when I am out with friends and away from my family, or shame because of the irrational fears that keep me awake at night. I live my life according to a never-ending shame narrative. It must be interrupted by a better, truer narrative: a story that we've been telling alongside the stories of shame—the story of God's goodness, of his pursuit of wayward and shame-filled and shaming people.

Start at the Beginning: God Separates
Our Guilt from Our Shame

Shame in the race we're running comes when we try to hold onto sin instead of letting it go. David is a remarkable example of a man after God's heart who knew deep forgiveness alongside deep sin. His sin (and its accompanying guilt and shame) could not keep him from God, because he regularly confessed it and received God's grace for it.

Shame is part of the more ambiguous category of "weight

that hinders." Guilt has been more clearly decried through the history of the church; shame is only now getting more "airtime." The culture confuses the two; it says that guilt and shame are the same, and that they are always unwanted emotions. The church has likewise conflated guilt and shame, with the effect of silencing those who struggle with shame with instructions more fitting to be rid of guilt. When a victim of abuse feels shame from her perpetrator, for instance, she does not first need instruction on how to confess her sin. She needs wisdom and courage to name the evil done against her as sin, and then to bring the lingering shame into the light of the beauty she is given through Jesus Christ.[1]

On our journey out of shame, we start with separating guilt from shame. The two are so closely connected that they easily mask and interfere with the other—with bad consequences. When I feel shame for getting impatient with my husband, it masks the guilt that rightly says I need forgiveness. I have sinned against God and my husband by becoming impatient and communicating my impatience through irritated words and tones and facial expressions. I need to start with repentance of my sin, asking forgiveness from God and my husband. Shame is what lingers even after I have confessed and repented of my sin. In this example, shame would insist that I continue to berate myself with the lies that I'm a bad wife for being impatient; that this is how I'll always be; that one day my husband will get fed up and stop loving me; that *God himself* is tired of forgiving me.

Shame comes with self-condemnation and a pervasive sense

of failure. Guilt arises over specific ways we miss the mark—God's mark—which, once brought to God through confession, disappears. David's words in Psalm 51 are the best example of what to do with guilt—take it to God! Realize that even the worst sin committed against someone else (in David's case, murder) is ultimately committed against God and needs to be dealt with in front of God (as well as the others involved).

To try to hide sin makes us languish. To confess sin makes us free.

Identify Your Default Response to Shame in Your Life

Once we understand how shame is separate from guilt, we can consider our default responses to shame. All of these are compelling, and we all have practiced them to varying degrees depending on the type of shame we have felt.

Hiding

Hiding looks like isolation from others. It can manifest as actual, physical hiding, but it can also take the form of creating an emotional distance to avoid intimacy. The Japanese use the term *hikikomori*, which describes when someone isolates himself indefinitely, removing himself from society out of shame: "Though acute social withdrawal in Japan appears to affect both genders equally, because of differing social expectations for maturing boys and girls, the most widely reported cases of *hikikomori* are from middle- and upper-middle-class families whose sons, typically their eldest, refuse to leave the home, often after experiencing one or more traumatic episodes of social or academic failure."[2] In Western culture, hiding can take the form of presenting an airbrushed version of yourself, the version you want others to see that's free of struggle. Hiding includes wearing masks like "I don't need anyone" and "I am perfect." We can even hide in plain sight by being surrounded by people and being involved in our communities, and yet not being transparent or authentic with how we are really doing. It's quite easy to hide behind an identity of "helper of others" and rarely admit our own need for help. To ask for help can trigger shame because it puts you at the mercy of another. It forces you to depend on others, and what if they ignore your request? Or what if they make you feel shame for having asked—for not being self-sufficient? Hiding *feels* safer than the possibility of being rejected or disappointed.

Blaming

When I feel shame for my failures, I'm tempted to blame you instead of facing and seeking healing for my own shame. Parents are the easiest to blame. Each time we feel shame, we can easily point the finger at the way we were raised and say that it was their fault. The same can occur when we feel like we are not meeting our own (unrealistic) expectations as a parent or a spouse or a friend. Instead of reconsidering our expectations, we blame those around us. We tend to confuse *triggers* of shame with *causes* for our shame. Parents, spouses, kids, and close friends may very well influence and provide occasions where we feel shame, but they do not *cause* our shame.

A notable exception is in cases of abuse and violation, when the shame of an abuser is transferred to the victim. Although the victim has done nothing shameful, she is made to feel ashamed because of what was done to her. If this is the source of your shame, you are right to hold your abuser responsible for your shame. Your tendency may be the opposite of what I'm describing here—you tend to self-blame when in fact you are to lay the blame at the feet of your abuser. Appendix B lists excellent resources that further address and detail the healing needed for shame experienced through abuse.

Personally, it is more common for me to blame others for shame I feel as a result of disappointed expectations, either mine or theirs. Remember my attempt to "vacuum up my shame," which I felt from a friend who visited our house? I was tempted to blame her and to find ways of keeping her from coming over, but as I considered the shame I felt, I realized it was my problem, not hers. I felt ashamed of my less-than-perfect housekeeping skills, and blamed her visit instead of examining the source of my shame. When I looked directly at my shame, I saw the ways that I was equating my value with the cleanliness of my home. I shared this with a friend who helped me take the first step out of this shame-and-blame cycle by reminding me that my identity in Christ has given me value completely separate from how messy my floors are.

Avoiding

I hope that by this point of the book, you are no longer avoiding your shame. Yet shame is easy to define as what "those people" struggle with. For me, as long as I relegated shame to the domain of victims of abuse, I could ignore those places where shame had gained a foothold in my own life. It can be easy to think of shame as arising only from particularly difficult struggles like sexual immorality or abuse. When we do this, we miss themes of shame in our own hearts, and we are hindered from connecting with others.

I observed this recently in a Sunday school discussion of the story of the prodigal sons. Everyone said they related to the older son who distanced himself from the Father through good performance, and no one admitted to relating to the younger son who distanced himself from the Father through wild, indulgent living far from home. Fascinating! It seems there is more perceived shame in struggling with "younger son" type sins than with struggling with self-righteousness, although both are equally spiritually dangerous and alienating.[3]

Indulging

The opposite of avoiding shame is indulging in the shame itself, or in the shame-inducing behavior. When we grow weary of fighting against shame, we often let it take up full residence in our lives, putting down roots into our identity so that we see ourselves as nothing but shameful. We proclaim it, perhaps through cynicism or an attitude of "Back off—I will hurt anyone who comes near me." We don't see shame as foreign, but as inherent to us. If you suspect that this is where you are, it will be particularly crucial for you to keep moving forward and to seek to separate shame from your identity.

Another way of indulging shame can be to give in to sin that you know will leave you with a "shame-hangover." This can be particularly enticing in addictive behavior, like compulsive eating or shopping or pornography or angry outbursts. These types of repetitive, self-destructive sins often are accompanied by shame on top of guilt. The battle to fight sin and seek forgiveness can feel exhausting, and the lie is that you might as well as stop trying and learn to live with shame as the price for your sin. But in giving up and giving in, you run the risk of indulging shame so that it melds into your identity.

God Frees You to Explore the Origins of Shame

Shame is a foreign body. We are not to grow comfortable with our shame, or adapt to it through hiding and blaming. Shame's ultimate origin is no less dark than the Accuser of our souls himself, Satan. Shame brings condemnation even after confession and repentance of sin. Shame says that there is more we must do to earn God's favor. Shame is a demanding taskmaster, calling for our attention but growing needier the more attention we give to it. Shame belongs to the domain of darkness—to the Evil One who always wants us to doubt whether we belong to the kingdom, whether God loves us, and whether we are truly forgiven and free of our sin and others' sin against us. Shame wants us to stay enchained to sin and cultural expectations.

Identifying shame's development in your life is crucial in your journey to becoming free from shame. Picture again the unhindered exuberance of a child dancing on a stage without a thought to whether she's socially acceptable in her mismatched outfit and out-of-tune singing. She is not thinking of others at all, seeing only her parents who delight in her because she is theirs.

It would be helpful for you to explore what type(s) of shame you typically experience, and chart its development in your story.

- What unfettered and free memories can you recall?
- When did you begin to feel the effect of shame and performance?
- Which people/events/experiences contributed to shame's development for you?
- Who counterbalanced shame's growth in you? Think beyond the obvious players like parents, siblings, and peers. Perhaps it was the kindness of a teacher who noticed your potential and your giftedness. Or a coach who applauded your athletic ability. Or a best friend who accepted you unconditionally when no one else had. Or a music instructor who encouraged you to play music for the beauty of it. Can you see and appreciate these people as agents of grace—used by God along the way in your story to give you a picture and taste of his love for you?
- What formative words ring in your head, forming the message of your shame?
- What current situations trigger shame for you?
- What expectations from yourself, your family, your church, or your culture do you feel you have failed?
- For what sins does shame linger, even after you have confessed and repented?

God Gives You Grace to Live according to a Different Story

We are to rewrite our shame stories moment by moment. First we must deal with sin through repentance. Once we have done that, we can speak back to the shame narrative. Using the example of my sinful anger, this sounds like:

- "I am not defined by my anger, but by who God has made me in Jesus—clothed in righteousness and holiness."
- "My sin doesn't get the last word anymore. Jesus took care of it all at the cross and triumphed over it in the resurrection."
- "In his death and resurrection Jesus silenced the chief Accuser once and for all."
- "I am loved, and nothing I do or don't do can change this fact."
- "The story I'm in is one of having been redeemed and made new; my destiny is nothing less than perfection once I am with Jesus face-to-face, when I will be like him."
- "Shame, you want to keep me separated from God and other people, but you don't hold that power over me anymore."

Read the book of Ruth, and notice the way that Ruth boldly and silently refuses the shame that seems to be her due. At each turning point, we see Ruth repeatedly identified as "the Moabite," which was a shameful term of exclusion in Israel acting *against* her given identity. Imagine the courage it took for her to follow Naomi's instructions to ask Boaz, a prominent and wealthy leader in Israel, to marry her! A woman cloaked in the shame of "outsider" and "widow" and "poor" wouldn't dare to be as bold as Ruth becomes on the threshing floor with Boaz. How does God describe her? She is a woman of virtue who is rewarded by becoming part of the lineage of King David, and eventually Jesus himself.

Another remarkable story of a woman acting contrary to her shame is Rahab of Jericho, who is also in the Davidic lineage and specifically named in the genealogy of Jesus. Her shame came from her profession as a prostitute. God rewrote her story, giving her courage to shelter the two Israelite spies, which would bring her salvation and a place with the people of God.

Passages such as the following can become infusions of courage to live according to your new identity in Christ rather than the old shame-laden self:

- "Therefore, if anyone is in Christ, he is a new creation. The old has gone, the new has come!" (2 Cor. 5:17).
- "There is therefore now no condemnation for those who are in Christ Jesus, for the law of the Spirit of life has set you free from the law of sin and death" (Rom. 8:1).
- "I [in all my shame] have been crucified with Christ and therefore I no longer live, but Christ lives in me. The life I live in the body I live by faith in the Son of God, who loved me and gave himself for me" (Gal. 2:20–21).
- "My life is hidden with Christ in God, and when Christ, who is my life appears, then I also will appear with him in glory" (Col. 3:2–3).
- "They glory in their shame, with minds set on earthly things. But our citizenship is in heaven, and from it we await a Savior, the Lord Jesus Christ" (Phil. 2:19–20).

God Redirects Your Focus

Shame most often arises from our perception of what others think of us—how they view us or our performance. We expect the worst from others, and we assume that they think about us as negatively and as much as we fear they do (which is not usually true). Yet even if their thoughts of us were as condemning as we fear, we are living for the wrong audience. As someone created in the image of God and for the purpose of reflecting who God is, I am created to live before God alone. By his judgment, I stand or fall. And because my life is hidden with Christ, I stand! I no longer focus on the people around me, who seem critical, or on a skewed perception of God as the distant judge, but on God as a delighted lover. In Christ, I am joined by faith to the eternal love of the Father. No more judgment remains—it was taken at the cross. If you're struggling with a perception of God as judging instead of loving, study his character as revealed throughout Scripture. Look at him for who he reveals himself to be, and so rewrite your misperception with the truth of his faithful love.

Romans 8:31–35 asks a series of rhetorical questions that bear repeating each time we feel crushed by shame:

> If God is for us, who can be against us? He who did not spare his own Son but gave him up for us all, how will he not also with him graciously give us all things? Who shall bring a charge against God's elect? It is God who justifies. Who is to condemn? Christ Jesus is the one who died—more than that, who was raised—who is at the right hand of God, who indeed is interceding for us. Who shall separate us from the love of Christ?

Bring Shame into the Light of Community

Shame thrives in secrecy. It gains momentum in our heads as it spins around and around like a pinball, seizing our thoughts and then our emotions. It tells us to go far away from others, especially God. When I run into shame yet again, it tells me I'm not worthy of being a parent or a spouse or a friend or a daughter, and so it's best for everyone else that I isolate myself. To follow shame's instructions leads us into saying yes to solitary pursuits and saying no to community and relationships.[4] Alternatively, shame can also lead us to overcommit and overwork in our obsession with covering up a lingering sense of inadequacy. It can be the reason we say yes too often. Either way, shame robs us of gospel rest. This Sabbath rest is promised to Jesus's people because he cried out in agony from the cross, "It is finished." When shame drowns out Jesus's proclamation, we feel like we cannot rest because our work is never finished, or rest becomes a guilty pleasure that we enjoy only half-heartedly because we are thinking about all the things we really *should* be doing. Or what we call *rest* is really lazy self-indulgence and withdrawal into ourselves in isolation from others.

I wonder if this difficulty with resting is part of why there is so much burn-out in full-time ministry. The story of Elise comes to mind. She gave her heart, soul, and schedule to full-time ministry on staff with a large church. As a single woman, boundaries between "time-off" and "ministry" became easily blurred since she roomed with a family from church and didn't have the built-in refuge of a husband or family. Her supervisor was blind to her needs because of the pressing needs of a rapidly growing church. Elise's desire to be needed blinded her to her own need to rest until it was almost too late. About five years in, she began having trouble sleeping, lost her appetite, and suffered from regular tension headaches. At a counselor's suggestion, she tracked the time she was working and lost count after fifty hours the first week. She requested time off, and spent the days sleeping or watching TV. After a month off, she returned to an evaluative meeting with her fellow church staff, and surprised everyone when she announced that she needed to quit entirely. It took months of soul and physical rest for her to be restored.

Shame was a restless taskmaster that contributed to Elise's overcommitment to ministry and to her colleagues' failure to shield her. Shame drives even (and perhaps especially) Christian workers to produce and to have measurable outcomes. Taking a purposeful rest or sabbatical can silence shame, at least temporarily, so that you can realize its presence and proactively fight it. Rest and community serve to remind you of your new, redeemed story.

We have strength through who we really are in Christ to live according to this new story, and to let shame be part of what connects us to others instead of a reason to isolate from others. We fight shame best when we talk to someone trusted about a shameful feeling, experience, or thought. The apostle Paul repeatedly boasts not in the many things for which he had reason to be proud, but of his weaknesses. He says in 2 Corinthians 12:9, "I will boast all the more gladly of my weaknesses, so that the power of Christ may rest upon me." Shame often shows up in the places of weakness that we want to hide from others, but Paul exhorts us to boast of our weaknesses so that Christ's power may be revealed in and through us. Christ's power propels us out of the hiding of shame into the light of authentic community through vulnerability, including brave, courageous truth-telling.

God's New Narrative Is Freedom, Learned Best by Practice

Freedom takes practice, which seems oxymoronic. Yet the only way to live increasingly free of shame is to practice living free of shame. If I did not feel shame about my body, how would I eat? Or exercise? Or dress? If I were not hyperfocused on performing for those around me, what would I do or not do? If I stopped thinking about who was or was not including me socially, who might I seek to connect with? What kind of gatherings might I host? When I dare to believe that God forgives my sinful anger and sets me free from the shame of not-good-enough that I always feel afterward, I can/am free to draw closer to my husband and kids and change the channel of my emotions from despair to hope.

Freedom does not equal perfection. As long as we have breath, we will wrestle with our own unique whispers of shame. The battle not to live weighed down by shame will be used to make us more like Jesus and to draw us closer to other people. Until I feel how hard it is to throw off the weight that hinders, I cannot be very empathetic when I watch you trudging along beside me in the race. Freedom comes as I fix my eyes on Jesus, realizing that the cross is the focal point where my sin is forgiven and my shame is covered. It is in fixing my eyes on Jesus that I learn how to despise my shame, because he was able to despise the shame of bearing *my* shame on the cross.

There was joy set before him, and so I can run freely after him in hope that his joy will also be mine one day. It makes even the heaviest shame-bearing days light and momentary compared to the weight of glory these troubles are achieving for me (2 Cor. 4:17).

What comes to mind is running with my college roommate, Katherine. It was the only season of my life in which I ran regularly, and the more we ran together, the easier and more enjoyable it became. She was training for a marathon, and I would accompany her on her "short" runs of three to four miles. What had felt burdensome at the beginning became light and easy because we ran together and because running with her helped to build up my endurance. If I had given up the first five minutes when I was out of shape and gasping for breath, I never would have known the joy of running freely along the prairie path together for miles at a time.

I think the journey to throw off shame's weight is similar for everyone. At the beginning, it feels as if we are slogging along and that the shame is more than we can handle. Yet as we practice running and living courageously free of shame in community with others, we will find that we are able to run farther, faster, and lighter the longer we practice throwing off shame's weight. And one day we will see face-to-face the One who's been beside us and in front of us all the time.

For Reflection and Discussion

1. What tends to be your default response(s) to shame (hiding, blaming, avoiding, indulging)? Describe an example of what this has looked like in your life.

2. Use the following questions to consider the origins of shame in your story. If you are in a small group, share some of your answers.

   - Do particular, formative words ring in your head, forming the message of your shame?
   - What experiences have felt most shaming?
   - What current situations trigger shame?
   - What expectations from yourself, your family, your church, or your culture do you feel like you have failed?
   - For what sins does shame linger even after you have confessed and repented?

3. When stuck in shame, how do you view God and others? What truth about God's love would help you to walk free of shame? Read Lamentations 3:21–24 and notice how God is described. If you believed this, what difference could that make today and tomorrow as you respond to shame?

4. How could you practice living free of shame this week?

7

Shame in Marriage

Set me as a seal upon your heart, as a seal upon your arm, for love is as strong as death. . . . Many waters cannot quench love, neither can floods drown it.

Song of Solomon 8:6–7

So far, we have explored a few key components to understanding and healing shame:

1. We all have shame.
2. Shame is different from guilt.
3. Jesus covers not only guilt, but also our shame through his life, death, and resurrection for his people.
4. Out of our new identity through faith by grace, we are united with Jesus and receive his righteous shame-free

performance in place of our struggling-to-cover-up-our-shame acts.

5. Walking out our redemption from shame frees us from: (a) body shame and obsession with appearance because we are clothed in Christ and made in God's image; (b) social shame and fear of rejection because we have an unshakeable place to belong in God's family as his beloved child; and (c) perfectionism, self-righteousness, and criticism as we rest in the work done on our behalf by Jesus and the perfection and eternal approval given to us through the life of Jesus by God.

Now we move into our day-to-day relationships. The next three chapters explore shame in the context of marriage, parenting, and church. What you have learned so far has tremendous implications for the way you love and relate to others, whether you are married or unmarried, a parent or a child. It is crucial that you do your own work before and alongside applying your shame redemption to these intimate relationships. Otherwise, the tendency will be to identify all the ways that your spouse or your parent or your child or your pastor has failed to appropriately empathize with you. You will want to blame any and all of the above for the shame you experience in your relationship. Undoubtedly, some of these past and present relationships have influenced and continue to shape the way you feel and process shame. *However*, focusing exclusively on these influencers in your story will not bring you freedom and healing. In fact, to apply what you have read so far *only* to others could result in more distance from them as you miss shame's true remedy.

A Tale of Two Couples

Jeremiah sits uncomfortably on the counselor's couch, listening to his wife, Samantha, berate him for the way he has not been the spiritual leader she thought she married. He recedes into the cushions, silently wishing that he could disappear and be somewhere else, or maybe even be with someone else.

Betsy's pain is written all over her face as she hears Jeff thoughtlessly recount the reasons why he was driven to an affair, and why he does not want to give up the love of his life, who is not Betsy. He begins talking about how it had been years since he and Betsy were sexually intimate, and because "she didn't meet my needs, I had to go elsewhere." She wants to cry, but no tears remain. She seems to have folded inward, like a sunflower at day's end.

These stories are not about real couples, but they could be.

If you're married, consider the following questions. If you're single, divorced, or widowed, think about your past marriage or a close relationship in your life. I hope that you will glean valuable truth from what follows. But if it's too difficult to read an entire chapter on marriage, skip to the next chapter on parenting, or the one that follows it on the church.

What is your marriage like? Has it been a source of your shame, or of shame's healing? I assume it has been both. Perhaps your spouse has inadvertently reinforced the shame messages you grew accustomed to as a child, but hopefully your husband or wife can be a powerful healing agent as you confront shame's insidious lies.

Let's turn the tables and ask the more uncomfortable

question: *Where have you been a source of shame and of shame's healing in your marriage?* It's easy to see the way that Samantha's approach only adds to Jeremiah's shame in his failure to be a spiritual leader (according to her definition), and the way that Jeff's lack of remorse heaps extra helpings of shame into an already shame-filled story for Betsy in discovering her husband's affair. But do you see yourself in Samantha and Jeff? And imagine Jeremiah and Betsy's feelings of withdrawal, receding inward. Have you ever noticed a similar response in your own spouse? Have you considered how you may be contributing to his or her shame-filled behavior?

A scenario not hard to imagine is that after the marriage counseling session, Jeremiah feels less motivated to draw close to Samantha and lead their marriage toward God. He now feels even more shame because Samantha has said these things in front of another person. When given the choice the next morning to hit the snooze button or to wake up and meet with his men's group from church, which one will he be more likely to choose? Jeremiah is still responsible for his response to Samantha's shame-inducing words, but she has made his struggle to be the spiritual leader she wants him to be actually *more difficult* through her berating.

Consider the second scenario. Jeff's prideful boasting about his affair and all the reasons why Betsy failed him will serve to exacerbate her shame and accelerate a likely descent into depression. The primary issue is obviously Jeff's unfaithfulness to Betsy. But if the counselor/friend/pastor does not also address the shame he's heaping onto Betsy, she could quickly go to a place of deeper isolation and shame, and her feelings of helplessness and invalidation will multiply.

Three Steps to Identify Shame in Your Marriage

Shame is written all over the stories of each of our marriages. I have been married for almost a decade, hardly a drop in the bucket compared to the legacy of my parents and in-laws' marriages of more than forty years. And yet these nine years have been long enough for me to feel shame, to exert shame, and to join together with my husband to begin to heal shame in each other's lives. Regardless of how long you have been married, or whether you are in your first marriage or your third marriage, it is not too late or too early to begin to address how shame has impacted your marriage, and how God's healing of shame through Jesus can begin to also heal your marriage.

Step 1: *Acknowledge* shame as an unwelcome guest in your marriage.

Step 2: *Own* the ways you have shamed your spouse.

Step 3: *Join* your spouse to be part of shame's healing.

Step 1: Acknowledge Shame as an Unwelcome Guest in Your Marriage

Because all of us struggle with shame in some form or fashion, including your husband or wife, shame will be present in every marriage. It's simply a question of how shame will specifically manifest itself in your marriage and to what degree. Consider a few possibilities:

Lack of Vulnerability, Honesty, or Empathy

- Are some topics off-limits, because you or your spouse get too prickly or defensive or embarrassed?
- Can you share embarrassing stories with your spouse and expect empathy, or would you be more likely to receive further ridicule?
- Do you talk about your failures openly, past and present?
- Is your spouse the first person you turn to for support, comfort, or celebration? If not, why not? Do you expect your spouse to be your biggest cheerleader in life? And are you the same for your spouse?

Lack of Confession or Forgiveness

- Do you confess your sins to one another as needed, as often as sin arises?
- When your spouse asks for forgiveness or confesses sin, how do you respond? Do you heap condemnation on him or her before offering a reluctant forgiveness? Do you refuse to forgive? (Note: In situations involving physical, sexual, or emotional abuse, this question becomes more complicated. It is worth noting that forgiveness and reconciliation are different, and that wisdom may very well mean forgiveness *from a distance* if you are dealing with a chronically abusive spouse. Refer to the resources in appendix B for further direction and guidance if you suspect that abusive dynamics are at work in your marriage.)
- When you confront sin in your spouse, do you do so with gentleness and humility as a fellow struggler, or with self-righteousness as one who would *never sin in that way*?

- Would you prefer not to talk about sin at all, because it's just too uncomfortable for both of you?

Lack of Intimacy

- How comfortable are you with your sexual relationship? Are you "naked and unashamed" as the Bible describes married sexuality (see Genesis 3 and Song of Solomon)?
- Do you share your emotions with your spouse? Does he or she share his or hers with you?
- When conflicts arise between you, are you able to resolve them or do you seem to stall out frequently when one of you withdraws indefinitely?
- Do you regularly share with each other what God is teaching you and how he's speaking to you through his Word, church, and your personal devotional life?
- Do you pray together often?

For step one, acknowledge the ways shame shows up in your marriage. Every marriage will have at least one or two areas of weakness where shame, rather than grace, rules responses. Now that you've identified them, you can get to work.

Step 2: Own the Ways You Have Shamed Your Spouse

It would be easy to go through the questions listed above and identify the ways that your husband or wife needs to change so that there is less shame in your marriage. When I wrote this list, I have to admit that my first impulse was to tell my husband, Seth, all the things "we" need to work on for us to grow in shame-resisting intimacy in our marriage. I could picture the conversation going something like this:

Heather (with enthusiasm): You won't believe the insights I gained as I wrote the chapter on shame in marriage. We have a lot of things we need to work on together; there are so many places where we can help heal one another's shame!

Seth (with cautious curiosity): Really? Tell me more.

Heather: Well, you know how I'm always asking you how you're feeling?

Seth: Yes . . .

Heather: Research proves that for us to grow in emotional intimacy, we need to be free to share our emotions with one another. So let's practice telling each other how we feel every night after dinner.

[*What Seth hears*: "You need to do a better job of telling me how you feel."]

Seth (sighs with resignation): Sure . . .

This would be exhibit A of how *not* to use the assessment questions under step one. Instead, identify the places where *you* have been reluctant or unwilling to be vulnerable and honest and the ways that *you* have not been a safe, empathetic support or refuge for your spouse. I guarantee your conversation with your marriage partner will go better if you begin with acknowledging your shortcomings and failures to love him or her well.

A formula for your conversation could be: "I realize that I have been shaming you through all the ways that I _____." Fill in the blank with one or more of the following:

- don't listen when you share something important
- have a hard time asking for your forgiveness or admitting when I'm wrong

- ridicule you when I see you fail
- dismiss you when you're trying to bring up a marital concern
- berate or condemn you for your sin
- make judgmental comments about your appearance or your work or your parenting or your housekeeping or your lovemaking

God's Love Provides the Courage You Need When Confronting Shame

The only way that you will have courage for such a conversation is if you are convinced that regardless of your spouse's response, you yourself are loved through and through—that you are known intimately and loved completely. Paul's prayer for the Ephesian church is appropriate for us at this point:

> For this reason I bow my knees before the Father, from whom every family in heaven and on earth is named, that according to the riches of his glory he may grant you to be strengthened with power through his Spirit in your inner being, so that Christ may dwell in your hearts through faith—that you, being rooted and grounded in love, may have strength to comprehend with all the saints what is the breadth and length and height and depth, and to know the love of Christ that surpasses knowledge, that you may be filled with all the fullness of God. (3:14–19)

When you are filled to overflowing with the fullness of God, there is little room for fear or for shame. God's perfect love drives them out. And besides, the alternative to *not* having this conversation with your spouse is living with the elephant in your living room that grows larger and larger and larger every day. Shame can erode your marriage unless confronted directly. Marriages can have silent, slow deaths of receding intimacy while maintaining the appearance of union. Let *that* fear drive you to engage in your marriage wholeheartedly.

Today you can begin the process of healing the shame you've inflicted on your husband or wife by acknowledging its existence. You can begin to practice love, the very love of Christ, whose love your marriage is meant to emulate. Your marital relationship is a flesh-and-blood representative of Christ's relationship with his people, and this is a relationship that heals shame at every level. So start with where you are, with the shame you notice right now, and address it courageously and gently. Consider Brené Brown's words: "Are we practicing love? Yes, most of us are really good at professing it—sometimes ten times a day. But are we walking the talk? Are we being our most vulnerable selves? Are we showing trust, kindness, affection, and respect to our partners? It's not the lack of professing that gets us in trouble in our relationships; it's failing to practice love that leads to hurt."[1]

If you are still unsure of how well you're practicing love and if you feel particularly brave, ask this dangerous question of your spouse: "What are ways that you have felt shame from me?" If your spouse stares at you with a deer-in-the-headlights kind of look, you might have to start at the beginning (and perhaps this book would help your spouse, too). Remember, your spouse might not be as far along in this journey as you are.

Step 3: Join Your Spouse to Be Part of Shame's Healing

If our model and power for shame's healing in our marriage is Jesus Christ's relationship to the church, then we must remember *how* God heals the shame of his people from their sin and the sin of others. Beginning in the garden of Eden, when shame first appeared, we see God healing shame by *covering* it with his pursuit of Adam and Eve and giving them better garments than what they could manufacture. Later the psalms give us an inside look into the way that the Israelites, God's original "church" (defined as people who belong to God through faith) processed their shame before God. Consider Psalm 22:4–5: "In you our fathers trusted; they trusted, and you delivered them. To you they cried and were rescued; in you they trusted and were not put to shame." David cries out in Psalm 25: "To you, O LORD, I lift up my soul. O my God, in you I trust; let me not be put to shame; let not my enemies exult over me. Indeed, none who wait for you shall be put to shame; they shall be ashamed who are wantonly treacherous. Make me to know your ways, O LORD; teach me your paths. Lead me in your truth and teach me, for you are the God of my salvation; for you I wait all the day long. . . . Oh, guard my soul, and deliver me! Let me not be put to shame, for I take refuge in you" (vv.1–5, 20). When the Israelites experience shame, or the fear of being shamed by their enemies, they cry out to God, expecting that God will answer with deliverance and refuge.

We know that God's ultimate answer to his people's cry for deliverance and refuge from shame was the provision of Jesus as our Savior to expunge shame at its root: sin. Jesus would be the shame-bearer to carry *both* the guilt and the shame of our sin into the "wilderness" (like the goat of atonement), thus delivering his people from it. Jesus would secure our relationship with God by bearing the weight of our sin and providing us with robes of righteousness (Isaiah 53). Jesus transformed our fear of God's deserved wrath by becoming our refuge *from* God's wrath. Shame cannot have the final say over you any longer because God has covered you and provided for your deepest shame: separation from him.

Therefore, marriage that reflects Christ's relationship with his people is to be a picture of this *covering over* of shame and *provision for* shame. In marriage, we have the opportunity to be completely exposed to another, and for him or her not to turn away in disgust or repulsion or rejection. We have the opportunity for another to be completely exposed to us, and to meet his or her fear of shame with welcome and acceptance and love. We are called to love as God did, and when our spouse confesses a shame experience or a shameful act, he or she should expect that you will be a safe place for him or her. A place of refuge. Maybe this means listening all the way through without judgment or interruption. It might involve asking questions to understand his or her experience further. Your spouse might need a secure embrace, or a kiss, or sexual intimacy as a physical reminder of your love. (Note: this may not be immediately possible, or even wise, if what is confessed impacts the sexual relationship, like an affair or pornography. See the additional resources in appendix B to explore that further.)

After the initial empathetic response, you may need to be

part of your spouse's deliverance from shame. Your empathy itself is a powerful weapon against shame—you've already started the process of offering refuge. Over and over again, God's people cry out to him about their shame, asking and expecting deliverance from it. They expect God to hear and to deliver. Over and over again in the Psalms we see evidence of God's deliverance. What could that look like in marriage?

1. Be on your spouse's side no matter what. Early in our marriage, an older couple modeled this for Seth and me. Mike and Suzanne wisely pointed out that we were acting like opposing attorneys in court when in fact *we were supposed to be on the same team.* The phrase "we're on the same team" has been a steadying call for us to redefine the enemy and to stand firmly alongside one another amidst life's trials and temptations. Together we have the chance to navigate difficulties and stress of work and home and relatives and friends. I get to join him when he shares about relational conflict, and he does the same for me. When we're in a parenting dilemma, we fight the temptation to pit one against the other and unconditionally support one another in front of our kids even if later we privately disagree. (Note: The only time this is not recommended is if abuse is occurring. You are responsible to intervene for the sake of your child's protection as soon as possible, and you may need to bring in outside help if it has become a pattern, or if you feel like you're in danger by intervening.)

2. Join your spouse in confronting someone who has treated him or her unfairly. If at all possible, you should encourage your spouse to confront the person alone first, unless it's a case of danger or abuse. After this, as per the pattern of Matthew 18, go with your spouse to confront this person. It communicates protective care for your spouse and that you are a united front. At times a woman seeking counseling will ask if she can bring her husband, an offer I always welcome. I've witnessed how a husband can provide tremendous physical and emotional support to his wife as she works through past abuse or an ongoing difficult relationship. It's a beautiful way he offers refuge to her. The reverse is equally powerful—seeing a woman be a source of strength for her husband when he's been buffeted by waves of criticism or by a past that haunts him.

3. *Do not allow your family or friends to speak badly about your spouse.* A friend of mine clearly told his mother early on in his marriage that he would in no way tolerate her continual put-downs of his wife. Too often a husband or wife does not draw a clear line in the marriage, with the result that parents have free reign to criticize, with potentially disastrous results that create a divide between you and your spouse.

4. *Bring your spouse with you to Jesus.* There may be times of intensive shame when it is difficult for your spouse to verbalize what he or she is wrestling with, especially in situations where he or she is seeking healing and restoration from sexual sin or abuse. He or she may need you to bring him or her with you to Jesus, like the friends of the paralytic who lowered their friend through the roof (Mark 2:3–5). You, too, may need creative persistence as you pray with and for your husband or wife and remind him or her of gospel shame-dispelling truth. Never underestimate the power of remaining with him or her

through the ups and downs of shame—which tangibly communicates real, practical truth of God's faithfulness to them. You cannot alone deliver your spouse from shame because you do not have *that* kind of power, but you can continue to seek strength to love faithfully through the one who *is* powerful enough to rescue him or her from shame.

What we are saying when we join with one another is, "You belong to me." And since shame's dominant root is the fear of rejection, this begins to choke shame of its best weapon and strongest fertilizer/soil. "You belong to me, and I belong to you. So come what may—flesh, Devil, death, world—nothing has the power to separate our love because it's rooted in the very strong love of Christ."

Limits of Healing?

Are there marriages where healing becomes impossible? Sadly, yes. The opening stories of Samantha and Jeremiah and Betsy and Jeff are stories of marriages that are on the path to separation or divorce without divine intervention. But do you know how that divine intervention can come? Through you becoming courageous and bold enough to acknowledge shame's presence and begin to strip it of its power through your willingness to name it and join together with your spouse against it. If you identify with Samantha, Jeremiah, Betsy, or Jeff, realize that you are at a crucial place where help is necessary and you cannot do this marriage work on your own. Asking for counsel from a trusted older couple or pastor or counselor is a very good place to start if you're not sure how to take the next courageous step away from patterns of shame in your marriage. In absence of that, read this book together and pray for humility to own your part and courage to risk vulnerability once again with someone who has hurt you repeatedly. And know that I still fall on the side of hope for your marriage because the outcome of God's pursuit of his bride was after *generations* of rebellion and spiritual adultery on the part of his people. Because God's love for you never fails, you can bring a kind of love that "endures all things" into your marriage (1 Cor. 13:7).

For Reflection and Discussion

1. How can shame erode a marriage?
2. In the marriage of Jeremiah and Samantha or Betsy and Jeff, identify where shame shows up and what it would take for the couple to fight against shame together.
3. *For those who are married:*

   Step 1: *Acknowledge* shame as an unwelcome guest in your marriage.

   Step 2: *Own* the ways you have shamed your spouse.

   Step 3: *Join* your spouse to be part of shame's healing.

Walk through these three steps for yourself, and then with your spouse if she or he is willing. What are practical ways you can together fight shame's presence in your marriage? What should you stop doing, and what do you need to start doing, or begin doing better or more often?

How well do you join your spouse? What's one practical way that you can communicate that you are with him or her in an area of struggle he or she is facing?

For those who are single (never married):
How have your friendships been a source of shame or of shame's healing for you?

Are there ways that you experience shame because of your singleness? How can your community, particularly your church, help you fight against this shame? Consider sharing this struggle with a trusted friend, or with your group.

For those who are divorced singles:
How do you think shame played a role in your divorce? Is there lingering shame from your marriage that needs to be healed? Are there ways you shamed your ex-spouse, and would it be appropriate to confess and repent to him or her?

Are there ways that you experience shame because of being divorced? How can your community, particularly your church, help you fight against this shame? Consider sharing this struggle with a trusted friend, or with your group.

For those who are widowed singles:
In reflecting on your marriage, where do you see shame? Does shame linger in your life because of ways your spouse shamed you or ways that you shamed your spouse? If so, seek God for healing and forgiveness, and talk through this with a safe and trusted friend, pastor, or counselor.

How was your marriage also a source of shame's healing for you, whether in big or in small ways?

8

Shame-Free Parenting

> The love that parents show to their children is a
> reflection of God's mercy. . . . Children . . . need to
> experience their parents' delight.
>
> Dan Allender

Does "shame-free parenting" exist? And what is "shame-free parenting"? Shame-free parenting is a way of nurturing your children through training, instruction, discipline, and love without relying on the powerful tool of embarrassment, while avoiding practices that for your children would induce or exacerbate their sense of personal shame. This implies knowing your children, staying emotionally attuned to them even in the midst of moments of instruction and correction, and also knowing yourself—where does shame have a hold on you, and how were you parented with shame?

It's important to remember the difference between shame and guilt. We want to teach our children right from wrong, and part of this comes from a desire to help them develop an appropriate sense of guilt. Guilt leads your child to want to make it right through owning up to a sinful act or attitude and asking forgiveness from the wronged party. It doesn't linger; it's a temporary state that can be rectified with actions of forgiveness. In contrast, shame is a pervasive sense of "I am bad, and there's no way I can fix what's wrong." It's also accompanied by lies such as, "I can never do anything right," and "I am unworthy of love." Shame causes a child to withdraw from relationship or to blame those around him because the anticipated disapproval or rejection feels like too much to bear. Guilt may also motivate a child to hide or blame, but once the wrong is out in the open, restoration occurs and the child expects to draw close to her parent again.

Now we begin to address the pressing question: *Is shame-free parenting possible?* Yes and no. Because we ourselves have been redeemed from sin because of the work of Jesus Christ, we are hopeful that we can parent our children in a shame-free direction, even if we ourselves did not experience this type of parenting. Yet we still live in a world plagued with the broken reality of sin's presence and power, which has a hold on our hearts and the hearts of our children. And they will encounter others in their lives who are as imperfect as we are, or "worse" according to our estimation. Despite our best attempts to raise them free of shame, they will have to face and work through shame from others until that day of redemption, as we do.

Although it's true that parenting without shame seems like an elusive hope, I still contend that it is worth striving toward.

Shame-Free Parenting as a Way to Battle against Evil

When we are under shame's control, we think about how to quickly get rid of it, and we focus too much on the opinions of others. We get stuck in the mire of condemnation and quickly sink into despair. Is our heart's gaze on God? Are we walking free in the hope that shame will one day disappear when we see our Savior face-to-face? Can we think about loving others? What is winning, evil or light? Regardless of the source of shame—our sin or that of others—to be stuck in shame is to be unable to receive and experience God's grace. This grace is always available to us, but we cannot hold onto it as ours because of Satan's lies that are wrapped around our heart and soul. These lies can sound like: "You're unworthy of grace. You will never be good enough for God or anyone else. You must do more to be acceptable. You are not beautiful. You will never be anything more than the sin with which you struggle or the failures that haunt you."

Of course, we as parents don't want to increase our children's propensity to believe these lies. We want to be parents who battle on the front lines for our children's hearts. We want to give them reasons to believe the unbelievable goodness of God's love for them, despite all evidence to the contrary. We desire to point them to a powerful antidote against the shameful experiences they will likely suffer in this broken world. Will we be able to do any of this perfectly? Of course not, but that does not mean we should not try. As ones who profess faith in a resurrected Jesus, we have the power of the Spirit available to us! Shame-free parenting begins with prayer—prayer that starts with confession and repentance of all the ways we have blamed our children for our shame, or the ways that we have thoughtlessly passed along the shame we have borne.

If you diligently and thoughtfully tried to parent without shame, how would your parenting change?

Consider these instructions: "Fathers, do not provoke your children to anger, but bring them up in the discipline and instruction of the Lord" (Eph. 6:4) and "Fathers, do not provoke your children, lest they become discouraged" (Col. 3:21). Could it be that God had in mind the discouragement produced by shame and its damaging impact on children when he gave these commands? It's an impact now being measured and quantified by modern-day parenting researchers, but isn't it true that God, who made children, has known this all along? Christians should lead the way in practicing shame-free parenting. Our children's hearts, as well as our own, demand it. The best way to fight evil is to proclaim the kingdom of light through our words and actions. This kingdom is characterized by the love of God the Father for us, his children, and by a love that leads us to imitate him as we parent our own children. Colossians 3:12–4:1, one of the household codes written to instruct Christians how to conduct their relationships within their homes, begins by addressing the readers as "God's chosen ones, holy and beloved" (v. 12). Following this identity are instructions to imitate God's love by putting on "compassionate hearts, kindness, humility, meekness, and patience," forgiveness "as the Lord has forgiven you," and "love, which binds everything together in perfect harmony." What apt instructions for us in parenting, providing a wealth of daily practical applications!

Discerning Patterns of Shame-Based Parenting

Our Savior, who loves children, says, "Let the little children come to me, and do not hinder them" (Matt. 19:14). Does our parenting allow our children free, clear pathways to Jesus? Or do we unwittingly block their way with shame-inducing obstacles? Consider the following questions as you evaluate your parenting style.

1. How often do you delight in your child? Joining with your children in an activity or play simply for the enjoyment of being with them communicates delight. For your teen, do you take time to participate with him or her in what he or she enjoys, even (or especially) if it's not "your thing"? Do you go to sports games, dance shows, or academic competitions with the sole purpose of cheering him or her on? Zephaniah 3:17 describes God's delight in his children, giving us a beautiful model to emulate as we parent: "The LORD your God is with you. . . . He will take great delight in you; in his love he will no longer rebuke you, but will rejoice over you with singing" (NIV).

2. Do you discipline your child publicly or privately? Public discipline exacerbates shame. Whenever possible, take your child to a private place: the car, a bathroom, or somewhere away from siblings.

3. When you correct your child's misbehavior, do you identify the act as separate from who he is? Consider the difference in the following: "Sammy, coloring on the sofa is not OK, and you are going to have consequences for that." Or, "Sammy, why are you so bad and mischievous all the time? You always get into trouble and do what you're not supposed to do!" If you're like me, it can be hard to think about what I should and shouldn't say when I'm in the moment of correction, so I offer you the chart below as a tool for your parenting toolbox.

LIFE-GIVING WORDS FOR PARENTING

Shame-Laden Words	Shame-Resilient Words
"You make me so angry!"	"I feel angry that you . . ."
"Why do you *always* [leave your dirty clothes on the floor]?" or "You *never* [listen to me]."	Instead of an absolute statement, point out the specific behavior. "It looks like you [left your dirty clothes on the floor] again." or "It seems like you're [having a hard time listening to me] lately."
Anything sarcastic	Be truthful about how you feel about what they did, or say nothing.
"I can't believe you [broke curfew] again."	"This is the [second time this month] that you've [broken curfew]. What's going on?"
"You are a mess!"	"You made a mess. Will you help me clean it up?"
"Don't you know better?	"It's frustrating to me that you keep doing what I've asked you not to do. Why do you think that is?"
"Don't act like a baby!"	Bite your tongue and say nothing at all.

4. Do you take time to cool down so that you're not disciplining in anger and frustration and running the risk of saying and doing things you will regret? Many days I have been the one who needed a time-out before either of my children did. Kids will push our buttons, and it is essential to learn how to calm ourselves down before deciding on the best course of action. They will also trigger shame for us. For example, the out-of-control toddler tantrum or teen screaming match in front of your in-laws makes you feel like a failure as a parent. If we don't identify our personal sense of shame *before* responding to our child, we run the risk of allowing our own shame to control the moment of discipline.

One parenting psychologist gives this warning: "We must practice choosing our words with grace. Otherwise our children—along with our spouses and ourselves—will bear the brunt of our careless words. . . . Harsh words reverberate. That's why I want you to promise to eliminate the phrases *Shame on you* or *You should be ashamed* from your vocabulary. Shame becomes internalized self-hatred. . . . So we have to discipline ourselves to make our instructions constructive."[1]

5. Do you affirm your love to your child before, during, and after correction or discipline? Children fear that their misbehavior has separated them from your love, so it's crucial to express the truth of the motivation behind your discipline, which is love. "Whether we're playing with [our kids], talking with them, laughing with them, or, yes, disciplining them, we want them to experience at a deep level the full force of our love and affection, whether we're acknowledging an act of kindness or addressing a misbehavior. Connection means that we give our kids our attention, that we respect them enough to listen to them, that we value their contribution to problem solving, and that we communicate to them that we're on their side—whether we like the way they're acting or not."[2]

6. *Are you tailoring your parenting and discipline to the developmental stage of your child?* For example, reasoning with a fourteen-month-old about why she should not touch the hot stove is usually ineffective (move her away from the stove instead!). So would be expecting your sixteen-year-old to spend all of his free time with his parents. Do some research on child and adolescent development—either formally (through reading books and articles) or informally (through discussions with fellow parents) to see if your expectations are realistic.

7. *Do you acknowledge and empathize with your child's feelings?* "Practically speaking, validation means resisting the temptation to deny or minimize what our kids are going through. . . . we want to communicate that we'll always be there for them, even at their absolute worst. We are willing to see them for whoever they are, whatever they feel. We want to join with them where they are, and acknowledge what they're going through."[3] When your child or teen shares something vulnerable or expresses emotions, how do you respond? Do you begin to minimize it, or dismiss it entirely as "That's so silly!" or "You shouldn't even care what that friend thinks"? Or do you make every effort to feel what your son or daughter is feeling in that moment? A simple way to connect emotion-

ally would be to listen and ask questions. The phrase "tell me more" covers a lot of empathetic ground. Another way might be to tell a story of when you felt the same way. Seeking to connect with their experiences, and especially when they're telling you something that feels embarrassing, shameful, or vulnerable to them, will help them not to be controlled by the insidious message of shame. *Connection expels the isolation in which shame thrives.*

Perhaps you've noticed that your child tends to respond with more of a pattern of shame than guilt when you've corrected or disciplined her, even when you've done so in a non-shaming way. Seek to point this out by describing what you observe. "You seem to withdraw from me after I correct you. Do you know why that is?" Depending on her age, giving her words to describe the shame could be helpful, such as, "Do you feel like everything you do is bad? Or do you wonder if I still love you?" Then you want to move from identifying and describing the shame she is experiencing to showing her Jesus as the One who's covered her shame. You want to give her the same tools for her shame that you're learning for your shame. So it would be a great time to remind her that Jesus died not only for sin, but also to cover shame. Because her sin is forgiven, her guilt is covered; and because she gets all of the goodness of Jesus's life through faith, God sees her with the same love he has for Jesus. God does not shame her or separate from her, and neither do you. Redemptive connection with your child after correction will go a long way in dispelling the shame that follows wrongdoing and failure.

Rescue Needed from the Shame Carousel

My struggle against shame-free parenting has largely stemmed from my need to calm myself down before disciplining my children. I never knew how angry I could be until I became a mother of twins. It began with desperation when faced with the overwhelming nature of two newborns' sets of demands for Mommy. I had the mercy of never fooling myself into thinking that I was adequate to meet my babies' needs, since their needs were often mutually exclusive. I felt the powerful message of shame that almost every mother wrestles with—that I couldn't do enough for my children, and that I was not enough for my children.

How did I respond to this growing message of shame in my heart? Instead of a growth in humility and repentance to seek help and admit my struggle, there grew in me a compulsion to try harder to be better so that I could become the parent I'd always dreamed I would be. I noticed a widening gap between how I wanted to parent and the day-to-day shame I felt when I failed my children. Anger and depression filled this gap—perhaps increasingly so due to the biological/hormonal factors as a postpartum mother.

Once my twins reached eighteen months and began exerting their wills in opposite directions, I responded too often with frustrated yelling. Afterward I always felt plagued with both guilt and shame. Anger had become part of how I shamed my children, and it was also a cause of my own shame. As a counselor, I knew how damaging a parent's anger can be, especially toward young children. My anger was important in sending me the message that I needed more than behavior modification or self-analysis. I needed to be rescued.

Rescue came as I reached out to a few good friends who encouraged me and prayed me through the hard days. I would text or call them, and they would respond with reminders of how loved I am by God and how God would give me strength to parent. Sometimes they would come over and provide a respite for a few hours. Other days they would suggest things to do, like going to a gym that offered free childcare or turning on a television show for a half hour, so that I could step away and remind myself of God's rescue as I journaled, prayed, and read the Bible. These friends gently nudged me in the direction of seeking professional help, too, through pursuing counseling and consulting with my OB about the possibility of postpartum depression.[4]

Your experience might be different. You could be more like Matt, whose workaholic father was distant during childhood. Matt's relationship with his father even as an adult was almost nonexistent, and it left him with deep messages of shame like "I'm unworthy of attention and love" and "I'm not important enough for my father to spend time with me." When he had children of his own, he began to spend extra hours at work instead of coming home, because that felt easier. He rationalized the long work days with the fact that money was tight, and someone needed to work. But when his wife pointed out the pattern of distance from her and the kids, Matt realized that he was unknowingly passing along the shame that he experienced from his father. Without the mercy of rescue, he would continue the cycle of passing along the same type of shame to his kids.

How to Practice Shame-Free Parenting

Most of us don't practice shame-free parenting not because we don't want to, but because we don't know *how*. I offer the following as a suggestion of how to begin to engage in shame-free parenting. These suggestions will likely expose the shame-inducing cycles of parenting in which we ourselves have been caught—so read these not as fuel for self-condemnation but as guidelines for seeking grace.

Know Your Child

God knows us intimately as his children, and we are to model this same knowledge as parents, as seen in Psalm 139. Love begins with knowing the other person. It is easy to assume that our children are just like us, and to try to fit them into our vision for their lives. Yet we must return to the question of how God has designed each of our children, and what he has planned for them. Here are some evaluative questions to ask yourself:

- What does he or she enjoy doing?
- Who are his or her favorite people?
- Does he or she tend to react to wrongdoing with guilt or with shame?
- What is his or her personality?
- How sensitive is your child to discipline and correction?

Action Steps

1. Pay close attention to your child during the day while he or she is engaging in play or in quiet moments, as well as during times of discipline or instruction. Ask good questions in order to engage your child at the end of the day.
2. Educate yourself on basic personality types and love languages, which is shorthand for how your child expresses and receives love. A few good resources are *Please Understand Me II* by David Kiersey (1998), *Personality Plus for Parents* by Florence Littauer (2000), and *The 5 Love Languages of Children* by Gary Chapman and Ross Campbell (2012).
3. Spend one-on-one time with your child doing an activity of *his or her* choice. It's amazing what you can learn about your child during these moments.

Know Yourself

It is wise to know the patterns of your own heart. As a coheir of God's gracious gift of life, knowing yourself leads you to know God and to love your child as you see yourself. To "train up a child in the way he should go" (Prov. 22:6) implies a working knowledge of the way he should go. Here are some evaluative questions to ask yourself:

- What is your default response to your child's misbehavior?
- What behaviors or attitudes tend to "push your buttons"? Are these biblical standards or personal standards? Do you communicate the difference between the two to your child?
- What do you tend to say when your child does something wrong? Do you point out the consequences of the behavior and why you disapprove? Or do you tend to make value or

identity statements such as "I'm disappointed in you" or "You are bad."

- Are you setting realistic or unrealistic standards for your children given their stage of development and your season of life?
- How were you shamed by your parents? What would it look like to parent differently? (Consider seeking pastoral or professional help from someone specializing in child development as a way to learn new tools and receive the support needed to change.)

Action Steps

1. Ask for forgiveness whenever you are wrong.
2. Admit your own failures as appropriate. It's good for your children to see that you're not perfect. Admitting failure helps them to let go of the idea that you expect them to be perfect.
3. Change methods of discipline and instruction to be less shaming and more productive. Be specific. Include instruction about how to do it differently in the future; include yourself as one who also needs God's grace and forgiveness for your own sin.
4. Never discipline for a childish mistake or an accident like spilling milk or not being able to tie his shoes or wetting the bed at night.
5. Study up on child development.
6. Seek counsel and help in knowing and owning your own story. Dan Allender's *To Be Told* (2006) and *How Children Raise Parents* (2005) as well as Daniel Siegel's *Parenting from the Inside Out* (2004) are good places to start, but

nothing replaces doing the work of understanding and owning your story in community with others.

Know Who Else Influences Your Child

You are the primary influencer, which means that you have the ability and the responsibility to monitor other influences in your child's life. First Corinthians 15:33 warns, "Bad company corrupts good character" (NIV). Here are some evaluative questions to ask yourself:

- Who else is spending a significant portion of time with your child? What messages are they communicating to your child? Do they tend to give messages of shame to your child?

- Who are your child's closest friends? Do they influence your child toward a positive view of self and God or toward a legalistic view of self and God?

- If you are not the primary influencer in your child's life, why is that the case? Could it be that your child is withdrawing from the sense of shame he or she feels in your presence? Are your children engaged in behavior that they know you don't approve of and aren't sure how to discuss it with you, or don't want to?

Action Steps

1. Be willing to gently approach influential caregivers in your child's life when you notice shaming methods. Suggest a different way of interacting—not in the presence of your child, of course! Show humility, knowing that you, too, are learning how to parent.

2. Talk to your older children or teens about their friends. Help them to be discerning with you by asking open-ended questions about their friends' influence.

3. When your children confess something they've done wrong, respond with love, grace, and acceptance. You can do this without condoning their behavior. Two parents whom I greatly respect told their teenage children that they wanted to hear about any misbehavior firsthand, not secondhand, that truth-telling was expected and their loving response was guaranteed. It did not negate consequences, but their kids knew that it would be worse to lie to their parents or try to cover it up.

Highlight Positive Behavior

Often as parents, particularly Christian parents, we are too focused on correcting our kids and teens when they miss the mark. We can see their misbehavior and bad attitudes more clearly than when they get things right. It is crucial for us to become detectives of their positive behavior, remembering that it is God's kindness that leads us to repentance (Rom. 2:4). Hebrews 3:13 instructs us to "encourage one another daily . . . so that none of you may be hardened by sin's deceitfulness" (NIV). Here are some evaluative questions to ask yourself:

- Do you focus only on negative behavior, or do you also draw attention to positive behavior?
- Would your child or teen be more likely to describe you as critical or as encouraging?
- Do you tend to praise one child more than the others? Or criticize one more than the rest? (Ask each of your children

individually if you want their honest perception of how well you're doing in not showing favoritism.)

Action Steps

1. Repent of your criticism (see the discussion of perfectionism in chap. 3) and find ways to be more purposefully encouraging of your child.
2. Notice even the smallest movements toward love, obedience, and kindness in your child, and verbalize it.
3. Be liberal and specific with your praise and approval, which is different from blindly praising and approving.

Trusting the Grace of Jesus to Interrupt the Shame Cycle

Let us conclude by calling to mind the only hope for an end to the generational shame cycles we find ourselves in as we parent. God the Father poured out all our shame on Jesus, who did not deserve it. All of our *own* shame and all of our absent or abusive parents' shame was borne by Jesus at the cross—in order that we could walk free of shame's insidious hold on our lives and our parenting.

Instead of trusting Jesus to convict our children's hearts and trusting God's grace to intervene in their lives as we lead them with us to his throne of grace, we tend to be quicker to identify places of correction rather than areas where our children obey and get things right as we lean on shame as a primary tool of parenting. We use shame in our parenting because we have forgotten that it's not shame of our sin that leads us to repentance, but it's God's kindness that leads us to repentance. "While we were still sinners, Christ died for us" (Rom. 5:8) is crucial to remember as parents seeking to live out the gospel that has rescued us as we raise our children and teens. Shaming doesn't rescue our kids, and it places more obstacles in their path toward grace. Picture instead joy-filled children growing into adults who are quick to extend and receive grace, who know their worth and dignity as ones beloved by God and delighted in by you. As parents, may we prayerfully seek to bring our sons and daughters along with us on our journey away from shame into freedom.

For Reflection and Discussion

1. In what ways was shame part of how you were parented? Or, if it wasn't, describe how your parents helped you to resist shame.
2. Where does shame commonly show up in parenting? Think about it in terms of parenting young children, elementary-age children, and teens.
3. If you're a parent, ask the suggested questions in the chapter to discern areas where shame-based parenting may have more of a hold than you thought. What came up as areas that need improvement?
4. Think about a time when God met you with grace after you had engaged in a behavior that left you feeling shame. How could you model this kind of love toward your child when he's experiencing shame?
5. If you're a parent, choose one action step to practice this week in parenting. Share it with your spouse or a trusted friend and ask them to pray for you.

9

Shame and the Church

The most powerful idea that's entered the world in the last few thousand years—the idea of grace—is the reason I would like to be a Christian.

Bono

Eva had always thought of church as judgmental—a group of hypocrites who didn't practice what they preached. But then a friend invited her to attend a new church in her neighborhood. What she found there was unexpected welcome and a love like she had never known. "They're my family," she often says with a tear in her eye and a huge smile on her face. This particular church has as its mission statement: "We aspire to be a community of grace, where each of us 'as broken, hurting, sinful people' find forgiveness, healing, and hope in Jesus Christ.

Therefore, we want to extend this grace to all, knowing that no one is beyond God's reach. . . . As a response to Christ's grace, we aspire to be a family characterized by love, joy, spiritual friendship, and compassionate pastoral care. Thus, we value ministry that welcomes children, youth and adults, both married and unmarried, into the family of God, where we enjoy each other and together delight in our Lord."[1]

I love this description because it's what the church should be. We are called to be a family, joined with one another through union to Jesus Christ and extending the welcome of the gospel to each other and to anyone who walks through our doors. As we all know, family is far from perfect—but family is known as the place where you can return and find belonging without trying. "Home is where your story begins" is an often-repeated cliché (particularly in the counseling profession)—and home is also where you should learn what belonging is meant to feel like in the context of committed relationships.

Eva's story of finding unexpected home and family in the church should characterize all churches. The New Testament Epistles address the church as a place where we practice love for one another out of our unity in Jesus Christ. Consider, for example: "So then you are no longer strangers and aliens, but you are fellow citizens with the saints and members of the household of God, built on the foundation of the apostles and prophets, Christ Jesus himself being the cornerstone, in whom the whole structure, being joined together, grows into a holy temple in the Lord. In him you also are being built together into a dwelling place for God by the Spirit" (Eph. 2:19–22).

We find these instructions from the apostle Paul to a new church in Rome:

> Let love be genuine. . . . Love one another with brotherly affection. Outdo one another in showing honor. . . . Rejoice in hope, be patient in tribulation, be constant in prayer. Contribute to the needs of the saints and seek to show hospitality.
>
> Bless those who persecute you; bless and do not curse them. Rejoice with those who rejoice, weep with those who weep. Live in harmony with one another. Do not be haughty, but associate with the lowly. Never be wise in your own sight. Repay no one evil for evil, but give thought to do what is honorable in the sight of all. If possible, so far as it depends on you, live peaceably with all. (Rom. 12:9–18)

Church is to be a place where shame flees in the presence of genuine community. Yes, it will be imperfect and there will be missteps along the way—family is often messy and hard—but we have the love of Christ, given to cover a multitude of sins. Forgiveness repairs the inevitable relational breaches, and grace leads our way back to each other when sin and shame isolate us. Yet when thinking of our Western society's view of the church, it has too often been defined by what it is against rather than the community of welcome it is meant to offer. For instance, words like *anti-abortion* and *anti-gay* come to mind more quickly than *social justice* and *a place to belong*. A recent study cited the overall decreased percentage of Americans describing themselves as Christian. Of particular concern in this study is the trend of those raised in the church abandoning faith when they get older: "Nearly a quarter of people who were raised as Christian have left the group."[2]

What could be contributing to this attrition? There are doubtless many factors, one of which may be the way the church has not adequately addressed shame, even at times being a source of more shame instead of less for those who need welcome the most. Consider Tom, a man who's struggling with depression. The consensus among professionals who treat depression is that it's a complex interplay of struggles with physical, emotional, and spiritual aspects. Some Christians take a simplistic view that depression always indicates sin. They are often well-intentioned, desiring to oppose the popular view of depression as only physical. However, would Tom be more or less likely to open up about his own struggle with depression if he heard a sermon, Sunday school lesson, or conversation to this effect? A place he hoped could be safe for him to struggle has instead added to the reasons he feels ashamed because of his depression. Imagine instead if depression were discussed in the church with compassion, acknowledging its complexity. Imagine if Tom met others in the church who were open about past or present struggles with depression and who walked alongside him as he grieved the losses in his story contributing to his sense of despair. Amidst such a compassionate culture, Tom would feel welcomed and more likely to share his own story. Healing could begin as he was woven into the fabric of the church's community instead of feeling like an outsider.

Jen Pollock Michel discusses this dynamic when she writes,

"Without grace, there is fear. And where there is fear, confession will be muted. Confession will always be unwelcome in places where authenticity engenders judgment and where we are pressured to conform and perform. Until we're allowed to be the mess we are, we will continue the hiding, the lying, and the pretending."[3]

The story of Jesus with the woman caught in adultery comes to mind. The Pharisees brought the woman to Jesus because the law stated that she must be stoned to death. Instead Jesus responded with, "Let him who is without sin among you be the first to cast a stone" (John 8:7). The response? They left, starting with the oldest to the youngest. There is much room for the evangelical church to grow in a similar response to likewise shame-inducing sins, like abortion, sexual immorality, and addictions. How could the church grow more grace-infused and welcoming? Imagine if the church were increasingly known for its reputation of decreasing shameful experiences rather than magnifying them! Oh, that Eva's story of finding unexpected welcome and grace in church were true for all of our churches!

Five Practices of a Shame-Resistant Church

A church seeking to offer a refuge from shame to all who enter will engage in the following five practices.

1. Church Leaders Talk about Shame

Preachers, small group leaders, Bible study teachers, and Sunday school teachers talk regularly and openly about their failures and struggles with shame. They use the word *shame* as well as *guilt*, and describe the differences between guilt and shame.

2. Sin Is Not on a "Shame Hierarchy"

The process outlined in Matthew 18 and Galatians 6 for confrontation and gentle restoration is in place for any sin that's discovered in the church. We are to confront others with humility and gentleness, seeking restoration without stigmatizing them simply because their particular sin struggle is more public than others. At its heart, all sin is spiritual adultery against God, and without the grace of Christ, none of us can fight temptation. At the cross, all sin is leveled, for we are all in need of atonement and redemption.

3. Sins of the Church as a Whole Are Examined and Confessed

Rather than confronting the sins of the outside culture, a shame-resisting church focuses more on repenting of its own sin. Romans 3 discusses not judging those outside the church while being brutally honest before God in confession of the sin in our own hearts. As we do this in a church, the atmosphere becomes permeated with grace; we extend the same welcome of the gospel to others that we ourselves have known. In this way, we follow the apostle Paul's teaching about letting the gospel alone be offensive. He talks about becoming all things to all men in order to save some, without adding any offensive obstacle to the gospel's proclamation (1 Cor. 9:22; 10:31–33; 2 Cor. 6:3).

4. The Response to Christians Who Are Caught in Public Failure Is One of Grace and Humility

Many Christians caught in public sin such as an affair end up leaving the church and the faith entirely. One could argue that they leave because this was the result of a faith lapse anyway, but what if one obstacle was the shame they knew they'd face if they returned to the church? It would be better to leave entirely than to have to confront the shame of what they'd done, they might reason. Brothers and sisters, this should not be! Yes, sin is destructive, but heaping additional stones of shame should not be part of the church's response. It suggests that we don't truly know the depths of sin in our own hearts if we can condemn someone else so easily. This kind of shaming attitude arises from the thought that "I would *never* do that." Be careful, we who think we are standing, lest we fall (1 Cor. 10:1). Christ himself was tempted in *every* way as we are, yet he did not sin. So if Christ could be tempted, who am I to say that I am above any kind of temptation another brother or sister will face? Because any of us can fall (and we do), we are to respond to another's fall into sin with compassion that seeks his restoration rather than seeking his punishment and exposure. Instead, church discipline often falls into one of two extremes: nonexistent or harsh and punitive. Biblical church discipline is always seeking to restore, and is enacted with compassion and grace. It is through speaking the truth in love that we *all* grow up into Christ (Eph. 4:11–13).

5. The Church Is First in Line to Welcome Those with Shame-Laced Stories

Those I counsel tell me stories that they have shared with no one else in the church because they were afraid of the response. I am often the first one to hear about an abortion by a seventeen-year-old, or a first marriage ending in divorce barely two years into it, or a same-sex attraction, or an emotional affair, or pornography. Any person whose story falls under the categories of sexual sin, abuse, divorce, self-harm, addiction, or abortion will have shame as a significant theme of his or her story. It will take time for them to trust someone in the church, and it is crucial that when this part of their story is first discussed, it be met with a response that exudes grace instead of shame. Are you ready to gently receive this part of someone's story when she finally dares to open up to you? To recognize her risk of vulnerability and meet it with empathy? Do you talk about these shame-triggered issues in a way that recognizes that the person you're talking to could have the same struggle in his or her past or present? Can you separate your thoughts and feelings about an issue or sin from the person standing in front of you? Realize that how you discuss shame-related topics says something to the person listening about whether you and your church would be a safe place for him or her to struggle, or whether he or she needs to keep following shame's contract of hiding and secrecy.

The Church as the Community of the "Wholehearted"

Brené Brown's shame research uncovered two categories of people: those stuck in their shame, and those whom she termed "wholehearted": people who do not let shame keep them from knowing they are worthy of love and belonging as they cultivate "courage, compassion, and connection."[4] Imagine if our churches were known as communities of the wholehearted. A gap in Brown's research is the definition of humans as made in

God's image, a concept termed *imago Dei*. *Imago Dei* is why we crave belonging, and it is also why we fear rejection. Author Hannah Anderson explains *imago Dei* this way: "When God created us in His image, He established a relationship with us that the rest of creation does not share. . . . Apart from Him, you cannot be fully human; apart from Him, you cannot be fully yourself. . . . In order to know yourself and exist as you were meant to exist, you must live in dependent communion with Him [and] be in loving relationship with others."[5] We know we are created to belong, first to our Creator, and then to fellow men and women who also reflect God's nature in their personhood. Yet the problem is that our connection to our Creator, the ultimate source of true worthiness, has been severed by sin. And if you don't talk about the fundamental human brokenness of sin, practicing shame resilience is like playing music on the *Titanic*. It may help you to feel better temporarily, but the ship is still sinking, and you are in need of rescue.

We cannot gloss over our inherent unworthiness arising from our sinful state. We all feel it in the reality that we can't even live up to our own standards for ourselves much less God's perfect standards as prescribed in the Bible. An easy glimpse is to evaluate how well you love those closest to you. The Bible says that if we cannot love the ones we see, how can we possibly love God, whom we do not see (1 John 4:20–21)? In place of love, we are indifferent, impatient, unkind, quick to hold grudges, envious, boastful, and proud. We exhibit all that love isn't, as defined by God in 1 Corinthians 13: "Love is patient and kind; love does not envy or boast; it is not arrogant or rude. It does not insist on its own way; it is not irritable or resentful; it does not rejoice in wrongdoing, but rejoices with the truth. Love bears all things, believes all things, hopes all things, endures all things." Substitute the word *love* with the word *God*, and we begin to get a picture of who God is—and the only person who loves like this is Jesus.

We are all stamped with unworthiness because sin makes us unworthy of such a love, and deep down inside, we know it. And yet in the greatest act of divine love, God came to us in our unworthiness and provided a substitute for our sin, teaching us to love while rescuing us from our failure to love.

Walking free of shame starts with seeing accurately our *un*worthiness and God's great worth.

We were created for perfection—to be like God—and we have fallen so far from this. Look at today's headlines if you doubt it. And notice the way you treat the person you like the least if you need more personal evidence. Read Jesus's Sermon on the Mount in Matthew 5–8, where he indicts us all by teaching that not only is it wrong to murder, but that being angry with another in your heart is like murdering him or her (Matt. 5:21–22), and that to practice your goodness in order to be seen by others cancels out any heavenly reward you would have gained (Matt. 6:1). We are unworthy of God's standards of perfection, summarized by Jesus in this same sermon: "You therefore must be perfect, as your heavenly Father is perfect" (Matt. 5:48).

God is worthy of all of our love, all of our obedience, all

of our worship, attention, honor, praise, and life-focus. And yet our unworthiness keeps us from worshiping him as worthy and blinds us from seeing his great worth. Our blind eyes must be opened. This is the grace of the Lord Jesus Christ for us. His rescue mission did what our feeble attempts to find our way back to God never could. He rescued us from the law, setting us free of the harsh and impossible taskmaster of sin, and he adopted us into God's family, calling us beloved children. Our identity is restored through the saving faith in Jesus to be what we cannot be: worthy. Then we are able to begin to see God as the worthy one he is, and to live a life of love enabled by the Holy Spirit. We are now worthy because we are hidden with and covered by the worthy Son, Jesus.

Our Great Worth: Inherited from Our Great God and Secured by His Great Love

Now we can face shame from a stronger place, a place where sin cannot pull us under by lies about our unworthiness. Jesus stands up for us, he stands *for* us, and he stands *in our place*. We are worthy of love and belonging *not because we have made ourselves worthy* but because God has loved us into his kingdom. With this unshakeable worth, the church has hope of being a community of truly, deeply wholehearted people. If sin cannot keep us from God's love, shame certainly cannot either. It's the argument of the greater to the lesser. Because God has taken away our deep, more indelible sin that kept us from him, then shame has no true basis to steal away our worth in God. For we who are in Christ, we always have the ultimate last word against shame. I am covered by Jesus Christ's righteousness. Death has lost its sting, the law has lost its power, and shame no longer has a valid claim on my identity.

I am worthy. Say it out loud. There is nothing you could do to earn God's love or to stop its flow from eternity past to eternity future. You stand firmly in the middle of this love tide that washes away shame. Shame's lies threaten to attack you at the foundation of your identity, but it is in that very place where you have the security of a forever love.

You are worthy, and you are in a community of fellow worthy beings. The church is a place where we find joy in our rescue and hope in the love poured out in our hearts through the Spirit. Therefore it is also a place where shame cannot thrive. For nothing is more powerful than a community's recognition of a person's worthiness. The church can drive shame away as often as it tries to slither into the cracks of our weakness and brokenness. For shame does not understand that these very places are the glue that binds us together, the source of our communal strength. Our weakness and brokenness serve to remind us of our common rescue and the abundant grace poured out into these very cracks so that shame is expelled. We are all simultaneously laid low and raised high at the foot of the cross; we are humbled by our sin and exalted by God's gracious love on our behalf. So shame cannot tell us anything about our inherent unworthiness that we have not already faced and been rescued from. It can do nothing to take away the love that guards and keeps us until the day of Christ Jesus when shame will disappear forever.

A Shame-Resistant Church Is Safe: Wesley's Story

We return to the question, What is safe? And how do we cultivate our church communities as places of safety? Consider the true story of Wesley (told in his book *Washed and Waiting*). He grew up in the church, never left the church or his public profession of faith, yet realized with dismay his same-sex attraction as he grew into adulthood. He knew the Bible's teaching that homosexual practice is sinful, and as much as it would have been convenient for him to seek to interpret these passages differently, he could not do so while continuing to live by faith in the Bible as God's Word, and Christ as his Savior. What was his option? For years he assumed that he must suffer in silence, carrying alone the shame of what felt like damaged sexuality. He tried to date women, but he was never attracted to them and felt this was unfair to them both to try to act otherwise. He respected other Christians who had stories of God changing homosexual desires to heterosexual desires, and he prayed earnestly that this, too, would happen to him. But years passed, and nothing changed except his desperate solitude. And so he took a risk in his early twenties, and he talked to a professor at his Christian college.

He eventually took greater risks by sharing with other believers and eventually fellow church members. Wesley describes his bold hope and intention: "No more secrets. I had tasted something of what it meant to walk in the light, and I wanted more. I wanted more than anything to see the church be the church and to know what it can mean to feel the freedom of openness and the consolations of community."[6]

What struck me as I read Wesley's story of honest struggles was the way that his Christian community, his church, embraced him in the midst of one of the most shame-triggering struggles of our day. He tells story after story of brothers in Christ who welcomed his confession, and who made themselves available to him during the inevitable moments of desperate loneliness by giving him a hug, praying with him, and being present with and for him. In this, not only does he show what courageous shame-defying truth-telling is, but he paints a picture of what the church can be amidst the battle against shame. We are to surround those who struggle most intensely with shame by offering nonjudgmental listening, perseverant and sacrificial love, and real, physical acts that communicate worthiness and belonging. We do so not out of pity, but out of our knowledge that we, too, have deep places of brokenness where shame would like to wreak havoc. The community we offer to others is the same community we ourselves need, too.

Those who came alongside Wesley gave him courage to tell his story and maintain his faith. This courage led to more bravery and more vulnerability, and more encouragement of the faith of believers who also know the burden of same-sex attraction. As he writes:

> Those who do bring their struggle to the light often confess that for years they kept it under wraps out of fear and shame. Far from wanting to contribute in any way to this widespread sense of shame, I hope this book may encourage other . . . Christians to take the risky step of opening up their lives to others in the body of Christ. In so doing,

they may find, as I have, by grace, that being known is spiritually healthier than remaining behind closed doors, that the light is better than the darkness.[7]

May, by God's grace, our own churches encourage such risk-taking and offer such welcome.

For Reflection and Discussion

1. Where does shame tend to show up in the church? What are the top issues or struggles associated with increasing shame in your church community?

2. If you attend church, which of the five practices of a shame-resistant church do you see in practice? Which could use improvement? How could you be part of the change?

3. When have you found welcome and acceptance in a church community (e.g., a small group gathering or Bible study or prayer group) when sharing a struggle, past or present, that you felt ashamed of? How did this help you in your struggle?

4. What strikes you about Wesley's story? Where do you want to grow in being more welcoming *and* in being more transparent with others at your church? If you aren't currently attending church, what would it take for you to give church another try?

Conclusion

A Shame-Free Destiny

And the King says, "Look! God and his children
are together again. No more running away. Or hiding. No more crying or being lonely or afraid. No
more being sick or dying. Because all those things
are gone. Yes, they're gone forever. Everything sad
has come untrue."

Sally Lloyd-Jones

Jake was in ninth grade when his trousers were pulled to his
ankles in the middle of lifting weights in a coed gym class.
He can remember and describe this incident like it was yes-
terday, despite the fact that he is now in his thirties and a dis-
tinguished professional who's received awards in his field. He
still blushes in the retelling of the moment, even when talking

to close friends who are all sharing embarrassing stories from childhood or adolescence.

Kelly shares about her abortion when she was eighteen years old, and tears well up in her eyes although she's twice that old now and has three adorable children. She admits that when she went through infertility struggles, she couldn't shake the thought that God was punishing her because of the abortion.

Debbie's sobs shake her body as she describes the process of grief from the loss of a close family member the year prior. The worst part for her is the haunting image that God is shaking his finger at her and saying, "You deserve this." Shame hijacks her mind, combining the experience of her harsh father with past sexual sin confessed and repented of long ago.

All three, Jake, Kelly, and Debbie, have done the work outlined in this book. They have named their shame, identified its origins, shared it with trusted others in community, and actively sought to live out of their new story of redemption through God's rescue. They believe that their sin is forgiven, and that their shame is covered. And yet the reality is that battling shame will be part of their lifelong faith journeys. Turning to Jesus and then to others brings healing, but they, like us, await full restoration and redemption.

Could this hope of a perfectly shame-free existence be part of what motivates them to continue slogging through the mire now? "Now if we hope for what we do not yet see, we wait for it patiently," Hebrews instructs us in chapter 11. Chapter 12 opens with the exhortation to fix our eyes on Jesus, who for the *joy* set before him endured the cross, *despising its shame*.

Could part of the joy he envisioned be the joy of shame converted to honor in the presence of God?

We know that there will be no more mourning or tears or death in the life to come. We look back to Eden to see that there was no shame before sin. Unashamed. It's where we began, and it is our destiny as the redeemed ones in Christ. The Christian's ultimate hope for shame is that we will be clothed in the honor of Jesus Christ when we stand before God in all his glory. Shame will be eradicated forever. No more hiding. No more past to haunt us—either that of our own sin or that of sin done against us. Shame will be thrown to the depths of hell where it belongs with the great Accuser of our souls.

Imagine standing before God unashamed, with nothing to fear because both guilt and shame are gone forever. No more wounds in need of healing; no memories of past sin to cause you to turn away from our God of light and his people; nothing at all to darken this kingdom where God is the one illuminating each corner of his new creation. It will be like emerging from a grim black-and-white film to a vivid and bright happy ending—an ending without end, that stretches into forever.

Jake is able to walk tall and act securely—no shame from past embarrassment haunts him. Kelly's shame melts away in the loving embrace of her Father. Debbie's joy at reunion with her beloved family member is eclipsed by the joy of God's delighted smile as he welcomes her home. She knows the truth that as far as the east is from the west, so far has God removed her sin from her (Ps. 103:12).

Honor crowns the heads of these three, and of all the saints as they rest from their labors—as they enter the kingdom where they are greeted with the warm welcome, "Well done, good and faithful servant."

Focusing on this sure and true shame-free destiny gives us hope to keep going—to keep battling shame's dark lies, to enlist others into our journeys with us, to seek to make our churches a small though imperfect taste of the life to come.

The Shame-Eradicating Power of the Holy Spirit

How can this be? Only by the Spirit. Our connection with Jesus through the Spirit erases the shame we've collected through our stories. The Spirit speaks through God's Word and his people, calling our bodies beautiful because we are clothed with Jesus's beauty; telling us that the striving of performance is over because of Christ's finished work for us; speaking into our hearts the words of forever belonging that expel the shame of exclusion. As we have together begun to find healing from our shame scars, we are able to offer the same to others in a way that transforms even and especially our most intimate relationships—with spouses, children, parents, best friends, roommates—and which spreads outward like the ripples of a stone thrown into a still pond. Our neighbors, our fellow churchgoers, our friends, our employees, and our employers are all relationships where we begin to honor instead of shame; where we are free to be unashamed of who we are; where we can admit failures and weaknesses and expect that these shame-defying admissions will invite others to courageous engagement of the same.

Fighting against shame moves you out of your lonely bunker of one into vibrant community. It does so one brave conversation at a time. It does so one relationship at a time. It will not be smooth and seamless. Expect your initial attempts to be flawed and broken and bumpy. You may test the waters and share something vulnerable only for it to be overlooked or dismissed (or worse yet, thrown back into your face). Remember that others are as imperfect as you are, and not everyone can be trusted with such a fragile offering. You will sigh with disappointment, and shame will want to recapture you by whispering that relationship is too costly. But then you will return to Jesus, and focus on him as the ultimate source of shame's healing. You will recall that Jesus, too, knows the depths of shame and the brokenness of humanity. You will take courage in his courage, and you will try again. It should not take long to find the "Me too!" response of empathy you are hoping for, which in and of itself rescues you from shame's worst lies of isolation. You will together celebrate that shame does not win—that it cannot keep you from connection. The shame that threatened to separate us from God's love and the love of others is the cause of deeper rejoicing as we deeply rest in our permanent adoption into God's family.

Our Destiny and Goal: Unashamed

The garden of Eden pictures Adam and Eve naked and unashamed before one another and before God. Sin marred the painting, leaving much brokenness in its wake, and shame was erected as a protective barrier between Adam and Eve and humanity and their Creator. Unashamed is an Edenic memory, yet it is also the destiny of those united by faith to Jesus. Jesus walked to the end of what shame fears: utter and complete isolation, separation from others and from God himself. By his wounds we are healed (Isa. 53:5). First comes healing from our deepest brokenness of sin, and then of all that flows from sin, including guilt and shame. We are healed not only of our sinful acts for which we feel guilty, but we are also healed of our innate fear of rejection and vague sense of unworthiness that clothes us with shame.

We have journeyed together through the ways that union with Christ by faith frees us from shame of all types, including body shame, performance shame, and social shame. We have seen how to combat shame in marriage and parenting. Amidst a growing awareness of how present and pervasive shame is in our lives and our world, we have explored a response to shame other than our typical defaults of hiding, blaming, avoiding, and indulging. We have been able to identify shame as different from guilt, to see where it began in our story, and to rewrite the shame narrative with an honored-in-Christ gospel narrative. We do not live for the approval or condemnation of others, but our audience is God himself—the one who calls us his beloved because of Jesus. Therefore, we move out freely into relationships without fearing or needing others' accolades or judgment. We practice our freedom at every turn—refusing to live according to shame's lies and awakening our souls to truth that sets us free.

This book is a fruit of my own journey away from shame

into the freedom of being clothed in Christ's beauty. I am a people-pleaser by nature and practice, and writing publicly terrifies me because of the fear of criticism and judgment. I want my words to be beautiful and perfect. And yet—like every other part of my life—they won't be and they cannot be. It is in offering my imperfect thoughts that I am practicing my freedom. It is in offering some of my failures and imperfect portions of my story that I hope to encourage you to do the same. Above all else, it is my unshakeable hope in the power of Jesus Christ to heal shame at its source that emboldens me to risk. For if you begin to taste the freedom of the unashamed in even one relationship, it becomes a seed that can transform your community. We need more neighborhoods, churches, homes, and workplaces where we live unashamed and give others space to live unashamed as well. Let's be part of the movement away from shame into freedom, honor, and glory.

For Reflection and Discussion

1. Describe the shame-free destiny for those redeemed by faith in Jesus Christ. Which aspect of this is especially appealing to you?

2. How are you living more unashamed as a result of reading and discussing this book? Where would you like to continue to grow in being free of shame?

3. "Fighting against shame moves you out of your lonely bunker of one into vibrant community." How is this happening in your own life? Where have you found perhaps unexpected community as you seek to walk free of shame?

Take a moment to thank God for that, and to pray for more communities, especially churches, to be set free to live unashamed. Ask God to show you where you can take the next brave step to be part of shame's healing on a community level.

Appendix A

Clinical Definition of Body Dysmorphic Disorder and Eating Disorders

At its extreme, body shame can become "body dysmorphic disorder," and perfectionism about changing body weight can take on the qualities of a life-endangering eating disorder. Body Dysmorphic Disorder is described in the Diagnostic and Statistical Manual of Mental Disorders (DSM-5) as: "Individuals with body dysmorphic disorder . . . are preoccupied with one or more perceived defects or flaws in their physical appearance, which they believe look ugly, unattractive, abnormal, or deformed. . . . The perceived flaws are not observable or appear only slight to other individuals. . . . Preoccupations can focus on one or many body areas, most commonly the skin, . . . hair, or nose. However, any body area can be the focus of concern. . . . The preoccupations are intrusive, unwanted, time-consuming . . . and usually difficult to resist or control."[1] It's when you cannot see yourself as anything *but* overweight, despite all evidence to the contrary (even when or if you are becoming dangerously thin). A close cousin is "muscle dysmorphic disorder," which is more common among men, and is defined as an obsessive focus on becoming more muscular and viewing yourself as less muscular than you really are.

Potentially life-endangering disordered eating patterns include "avoidant/restrictive food intake disorder, anorexia nervosa, bulimia nervosa, and binge-eating disorder."[2] One end of the spectrum is binge eating, and the other is anorexia, characterized by restrictive eating to the point of self-starvation. Women and men caught in the throes of anorexia or bulimia are often the last ones to admit it, and in fact, usually *cannot* see it until a friend, family member, physician, or counselor notices and invites them to seek help. If you're wondering if this is you, the first place to go is to a doctor for a medical evaluation. It takes tremendous courage to take this step, and you will likely need the support of a trusted friend, family member, pastor, or counselor. This first step of asking for help is the hardest but the most crucial.

It is also the most courageous.

Self-Evaluative Questions Worth Asking Yourself

1. Do I have rules for eating, such as eating only certain types and amounts of food in a given day, week, or season?
2. Do I enjoy cooking for others, but never eat anything that I prepare?

3. Do I eat past the point of hunger and binge on a huge amount of food?[3]

4. Have I experienced weight loss in a short period of time, cessation of menstruation without physiological cause, or dizziness or fainting spells? Or have I experienced frequent weight fluctuations or weight gain related to my eating/bingeing/purging habits?

5. Is my self-worth determined by my weight, dress size, or how self-controlled I've been about diet and exercise?[4]

If you answered yes to *any of these questions*, please seek help, as it could indicate the presence of an eating disorder (anorexia, bulimia, or binge eating).

Appendix B

Further Resources on Abuse

Sexual Abuse

Dan Allender, *The Wounded Heart: Hope for Adult Victims of Childhood Sexual Abuse* (Colorado Springs: NavPress, 1990).

Justin S. Holcomb and Lindsey A. Holcomb, *Rid of My Disgrace: Hope and Healing for Victims of Sexual Assault* (Wheaton, IL: Crossway, 2011).

Diane Mandt Langberg, *On the Threshold of Hope: Opening the Door to Healing for Survivors of Sexual Abuse* (Wheaton, IL: Tyndale, 1999).

Steven R. Tracy, *Mending the Soul: Understanding and Healing Abuse* (Grand Rapids, MI: Zondervan, 2005).

Suspected Abuse in Marriage or Child Abuse in the Home or Church

Childhelp hotline: 1-800-422-4453, www.childhelp.org.

National Domestic Violence Hotline: 1-800-799-7233.

Brenda Branson and Paula J. Silva, *Violence among Us: Ministry to Families in Crisis* (Valley Forge, PA: Judson Press, 2007).

David Powlison, *Recovering from Child Abuse: Healing and Hope for Victims*, CCEF website, http://www.ccef.org/resources /minibooks/recovering-child-abuse-healing-and-hope-victims.

Deepak Reju, *On Guard: Preventing and Responding to Child Abuse at Church* (Greensboro, NC: New Growth Press, 2014).

"Signs of Abuse and Abusive Relationships," HelpGuide.org, http://www.helpguide.org/articles/abuse/domestic-violence -and-abuse.htm.

Leslie Vernick, *The Emotionally Destructive Marriage* (Colorado Springs: WaterBrook Press, 2013).

———, *The Emotionally Destructive Relationship: Seeing It, Stopping It, Surviving It* (Eugene, OR: Harvest House, 2007).

Notes

Introduction: Shame: Everyone Has It

1. Brené Brown in *Daring Greatly: How the Courage to Be Vulnerable Transforms the Way We Live, Love, Parent, and Lead* illustrates the way men experience shame differently than women (New York: Penguin, 2012), 83–85.

2. "The stories of our struggles are difficult for everyone to own, and if we've worked hard to make sure everything looks 'just right' on the outside, the stakes are high when it comes to truth-telling. This is why shame loves perfectionists—it's so easy to keep us quiet." Brené Brown, *The Gifts of Imperfection: Let Go of Who You Think You're Supposed to Be and Embrace Who You Are* (Center City, MN: Hazelden, 2010), 39.

3. Brené Brown has written several *New York Times* bestsellers, including *The Gifts of Imperfection* (2010), *Daring Greatly* (2012), and *Rising Strong* (2015). See also her TEDx talks "Listening to Shame" (March 2012) and "The Power of Vulnerability" (June 2010): http://www.ted.com/talks/brene_brown _listening_to_shame?language=en/; http://www.ted.com/talks/brene_brown_on _vulnerability?language=en/.

4. Brown, *Daring Greatly*, 71.

5. Edward T. Welch, *Shame Interrupted: How God Lifts the Pain of Worthlessness and Rejection* (Greensboro: New Growth Press, 2012), 3.

6. Ibid., 11. Emphasis added.

7. Ibid. Emphasis added.

8. Brené Brown, "The Power of Vulnerability."

Chapter 2: Living Shamelessly through Christ-Formed Community

1. Brené Brown, *The Gifts of Imperfection: Let Go of Who You Think You're Supposed to Be and Embrace Who You Are* (Center City, MN: Hazelden, 2010), 19–20, quoting Daniel Goleman, *Social Intelligence: The New Science of Human Relationships* (New York: Random House, 2006).

2. Henry Cloud and John Townsend, *Safe People* (Grand Rapids, MI: Zondervan, 1995), 145–46.

3. Ray Ortlund, *The Gospel: How the Church Portrays the Beauty of Christ* (Wheaton, IL: Crossway, 2014), 72.
4. Google, s.v. "hospitality," accessed January 12, 2016, https://www.google.com/#q=hospitality.
5. *Dictionary.com*, s.v. "hospitality," accessed January 12, 2016, http://dictionary.reference.com/browse/hospitality?s=t.
6. For extended study on this topic of loving people instead of fearing/pleasing people, I recommend reading Ed Welch's *When People Are Big and God Is Small: Overcoming Peer Pressure, Codependency, and the Fear of Man* (Phillipsburg, NJ: P&R, 1997).

Chapter 3: Clothed in Christ

1. Michael Brodeur, "Why Male Body Shaming Is on the Rise in the Media," *Boston Globe*, March 8, 2015, https://www.bostonglobe.com/lifestyle/2015/03/08/manshaming/F4IOidjmYSzlbTvMGua0sJ/story.html#/.
2. National Eating Disorders Association, http://www.nationaleatingdisorders.org/get-facts-eating-disorders/.
3. "High Debt Correlates Strongly with Anxiety and Depression," reports Derek Thompson in "The 10 Things Economics Can Tell Us about Happiness," May 31, 2012, http://www.theatlantic.com/business/archive/2012/05/the-10-things-economics-can-tell-us-about-happiness/257947/.
4. *Dictionary.com*, s.v. "intricate," accessed November 16, 2015, http://dictionary.reference.com/browse/intricate?s=ts.
5. For further reading, see my article "Chasing Beauty," *Journal of Biblical Counseling*, no. 1 (winter 2006): 58–60.
6. I am indebted to my pastor, Rev. Jack Howell at Trinity Presbyterian Church (Norfolk, VA), who often includes in his sermons these heart-piercing questions contrasting idols of the heart with Jesus.

Chapter 4: United to Christ

1. Janet Morahan-Martin and Phyllis Schumacher, "Loneliness and Social Uses of the Internet," *Science Direct*, May 3, 2003, http://www.sciencedirect.com/science/article/pii/S0747563203000402.
2. Emily Freeman, *Grace for the Good Girl* (Grand Rapids, MI: Revell, 2011), 84, 92.
3. C. S. Lewis, *The Four Loves* (New York: Harcourt, Brace 1960), 169.
4. Brené Brown, *The Gifts of Imperfection: Let Go of Who You Think You're Supposed to Be and Embrace Who You Are* (Center City, MN: Hazelden, 2010), 25.
5. John Calvin, *Institutes of the Christian Religion*, ed. John T. McNeill, trans. Ford Lewis Battles (Philadelphia: Westminster, 1960), 1.1.1.
6. Elizabeth Gilbert, *Eat, Pray, Love: One Woman's Search for Everything across Italy, India, and Indonesia* (New York: Penguin, 2007).
7. Andy Crouch, "The Good News about Shame," *Christianity Today* (March 2015): 37.
8. Ed Welch, *Shame Interrupted: How God Lifts the Pain of Worthlessness and Rejection* (Greensboro, NC: New Growth Press, 2012), 229.

9. Matthew Sparkes, "Twitter and Facebook 'Addicts' Suffer Withdrawal Symptoms," *The Telegraph*, April 11, 2013, which cites a 2013 University of Winchester study, http://www.telegraph.co.uk/technology/social-media/9986950 /Twitter-and-Facebook-addicts-suffer-withdrawal-symptoms.html.

Chapter 5: Free in Christ

1. Brené Brown, *Daring Greatly: How the Courage to Be Vulnerable Transforms the Way We Live, Love, Parent, and Lead* (New York, Penguin, 2012), 135.
2. Ibid., 129.
3. D. A. Carson, "Leaning forward in the Dark: A Failed Reformation (Nehemiah 13)," The Gospel Coalition's 2014 National Women's Conference, June 29, 2014, http://resources.thegospelcoalition.org/library/leaning-forward-in-the -dark/.
4. A phrase marked by a hashtag (#) on social media is a way of linking to other pictures or thoughts in the same theme. This is most often used on Instagram and Twitter.
5. Emily Freeman, *A Million Little Ways* (Grand Rapids, MI: Revell, 2013), 29.
6. Glennon Doyle Melton, *Carry On, Warrior: The Power of Embracing Your Messy, Beautiful Life* (New York: Scribner, 2013), 242.

Chapter 6: Response to Shame

1. For an in-depth treatment of how to walk alongside a survivor of sexual abuse, or how to do so for yourself, I highly recommend Diane Langberg's book and its accompanying workbook, *On the Threshold of Hope* (Carol Stream, IL: Tyndale, 1999).
2. I first heard the term *hikikomori* from missionaries Bob and Sharon Drews while they were serving in Japan with Mission to the World. The quote is from *Wikipedia's* definition, http://en.wikipedia.org/wiki/Hikikomori/.
3. I am indebted to the teaching of Timothy Keller, a minister in New York City, on this topic—particularly in his book, *The Prodigal God: Recovering the Heart of the Christian Faith* (New York: Penguin, 2008).
4. Examples abound in our Western individualistic society of solitary pursuits that range from activities that aren't intrinsically harmful or damaging like reading, sleeping, watching TV or movies, exercise, shopping, and gaming to the always destructive addictions to pornography, drugs, and alcohol. If you're unsure of whether your solitary pursuits have crossed the line from healthy self-care and spiritual/physical engagement of the good gifts found in our created world, seek the input of a safe and trusted friend, family member, pastor, small group leader, or professional counselor.

Chapter 7: Shame in Marriage

1. Brené Brown, *Daring Greatly: How the Courage to Be Vulnerable Transforms the Way We Live, Love, Parent, and Lead* (New York: Penguin, 2012), 106–7.

Chapter 8: Shame-Free Parenting

1. Robin Berman, *Permission to Parent: How to Raise Your Child with Love and Limits* (New York: Harper Collins, 2014), 101, 110.

2. Daniel Siegel and Tina Payne Bryson, *No Drama Discipline: The Whole-Brain Way to Calm the Chaos and Nurture Your Child's Developing Mind* (New York: Random House, 2014), xxii.
3. Ibid., 127.
4. If you have any question about whether you are experiencing postpartum depression (which can present itself up to two years after delivery), seek medical and professional help as soon as you can. Your OB or midwife is the best starting place, as they are experts in recognizing and treating postpartum depression.

Chapter 9: Shame and the Church
1. Cresheim Valley Church, http://www.cvcpca.org/.
2. Nate Cohn, "Big Drop in Share of Americans Calling Themselves Christians," *The New York Times*, May 12, 2015, http://www.nytimes.com/2015/05/12/up shot/big-drop-in-share-of-americans-calling-themselves-christian.html/.
3. Jen Pollock Michel, *Teach Us to Want: Longing, Ambition, and the Life of Faith* (Downers Grove, IL: InterVarsity Press, 2014), 149.
4. Brené Brown, *The Gifts of Imperfection* (Center City, MN: Hazelden, 2010), 125.
5. Hannah Anderson, *Made for More* (Chicago: Moody, 2014), 34, 40.
6. Wesley Hill, *Washed and Waiting: Reflections on Christian Faithfulness and Homosexuality* (Grand Rapids, MI: Zondervan, 2010), 45.
7. Ibid., 17.

Appendix A: Clinical Definition of Body Dysmorphic Disorder and Eating Disorders
1. "Body Dysmorphic Disorder," *DSM-5* (Arlington, VA: American Psychiatric Association, 2013), 243.
2. "Feeding and Eating Disorders," *DSM-5* (Arlington, VA: American Psychiatric Association, 2013), 329.
3. Questions 1–3 are adapted from Jenni Schaefer, *Life without Ed: How One Woman Declared Independence from Her Eating Disorder and How You Can Too* (New York: McGraw-Hill Education, 2014), 59.
4. Questions 4–5 are adapted from Michele Siegel, Judith Brisman, and Margot Weinshel, *Surviving an Eating Disorder: Strategies for Family and Friends* (New York: Harper Perennial, 2009), 35–37.

General Index

Scripture Index